Yours To Design:

Constructing a Life That is Meaningful

YOURS TO DESIGN: CONSTRUCTING A LIFE THAT IS MEANINGFUL/DEANGELO BURSE
Published by Jehashi Publishing

ISBN: 979-8-9902796-8-1
Copyright © 2024 by DeAngelo Burse
Cover design by Rizwana k(Ridzz)
Interior design by atritex.com

Available in print from your local bookstore, online, or from the publisher.

For more information on this book and the author visit: deangeloburse.com

Library of Congress Cataloging-in-Publication Data
Burse, DeAngelo.
Yours To Design: Constructing A Life That Is Meaningful / DeAngelo Burse 1st ed.

Printed in the United States of America

To My Kids

This book is dedicated to my kids, Jenesis, Haven, and Cadence. If I were to try to inspire others without first being an inspiration to you, my work would be severely handicapped, contradictory, and hollow. I urge each of you never to forget that you can play an active role in shaping who you become and constructing a meaningful life. Always remember that I love you more than...

Thank You

I want to express my gratitude to all those who had a direct hand in bringing my book to completion.

To begin with, I would like to thank my wife, Teah, for her unwavering support and sacrifices throughout my entrepreneurial ventures, particularly in writing this book. She has been a pillar of strength, listening to my ideas and offering insight, providing feedback on early manuscript drafts, and constantly motivating me during moments of self-doubt. In addition, I'd like to thank my editor, Diana Flegal, who began as my agent and believed in me from the start. She has helped enhance my writing skills and played a pivotal role in elevating the quality of my book.

Furthermore, I'd like to express my gratitude to my mentors, Mark Leary and Norman Cotterell. I greatly appreciate Mark's meticulous editing and subject matter expertise, which often made me delve deeper into the concepts used in the book. I am also grateful for Norman's commitment to keep me accountable with my writing schedule, reading my manuscript back to me during our meetings, and providing feedback.

Next, I'd like to extend a heartfelt thank you to David Jones for his support in bringing this book to fruition. His constant inspiration and willingness to help have been invaluable. I'd also like to thank my friend Dion Baker for frequently listening to and encouraging ideas about my work, including some of those found in the book. Finally, I want to thank Eddie Jones, the project manager who played a crucial role in simplifying and executing the final steps of the process, ultimately leading to the publication of my book.

Contents

Preface

Do you ever sit and reflect on who you are, your career, your family, and each previous milestone that has brought you to this point in your life? I do this regularly, but I am always surprised how many people never consider these important questions: why am I the way I am, and how did I get to this point in life?

As a kid, you likely had vivid dreams about your future self and where you would go in life. Researchers agree that our imagination decreases with age. Still, I'm curious if the increasing complexity of our lives and negative experiences throughout adolescence and adulthood are partly to blame for the decline in imagination. It's no secret that competing priorities can strain our mental resources. I used to want to be a football player and then a musician—but then life threw me some curve balls, and I stopped focusing on my goals. As a result, I found myself working jobs and having relationships in my early twenties that I didn't particularly enjoy. I was so unhappy. Maybe you're feeling the same frustration right now.

Sunday became depressing because I had to go to my dreaded job on Monday, which set up an exhausting race to Friday. Friday became like Christmas Eve, leading to Christmas Saturday and then to depressing Sunday. This cycle continued like an agonizing broken record. I felt like the subject of a CIA black site interrogation, spending some Sunday evenings crying on the floor, begging God to make Monday feel like Friday and Tuesday feel like Saturday. I didn't want my emotions to fluctuate on different days of the week; I wanted every day to feel the same. I began the week without motivation, pushed myself through, and exhaled late Friday afternoon, hoping to find rest for a day or two before it all started again. Oh, and thank God for the long holiday weekends. You may be experiencing something similar.

Even as I struggled to find happiness and meaning, I believed that life was meant to be meaningful, and my motivation and emotions shouldn't be tied to specific days of the week. When I was in my late twenties, I began to see an answer to my prayer. Today, in my mid-40s, I feel complete, and I'm able to live and chase my dreams. In general, every day feels the same—purposeful. That's not to say I don't have bad days like everyone else, but most of them are equally meaningful. However, my journey to this new life and new me demanded a lengthy period of self-reflection, self-confrontation, self-determination, and faith. It required me to consider the two critical questions: "Why am I the way I am?" and "How did I arrive at this place in my life?"

In addition, I took bold action steps. It became apparent that the pain of keeping things the same was greater than the discomfort associated with change. The unknown risks, anxiety and fear, gossip and threats to my reputation, loss of friendships and relationships, and financial uncertainties were insignificant compared to the internal agony of feeling like my life was meaningless.

I searched for meaning encompassing who I was and where I was going. The idea that I had grown into the person I had become and haphazardly arrived at my place in life terrified me. Living without consistent thought about who we're becoming and without deliberate planning can have serious consequences, a process that's like rolling the dice on our future. Meaning can be attained only through intentionality, whereas meaninglessness is caused by randomness. It's no surprise that I had developed a sense of emptiness, given that much of my time was filled with random activities. Maybe this is how you feel right now: empty or somewhat unfulfilled. Then again, perhaps you're a life-long learner who just wants to grow.

Either way, we all fall into one of the following three categories: we've rolled the dice and don't like who we have become or where we are in life, or we have had some lucky rolls and aren't too worried about who we are or where we are going. Thirdly, we have been deliberate in our growth and like where we are in life but recognize we can always do better. Whatever the case may be, this book is for you.

There is a strong connection between who we are, where we are, and the stories we've told ourselves. Obviously, we can't control everything that happens to us; factors beyond our control can influence where we sometimes land, but who we become is within our control. I've met people who want to change for the better but simply don't know how. I've also met people who need to change but aren't aware of it. Have you ever heard the saying you don't know what you don't know? This book is designed to help you learn what you don't know.

This book is not meant to offer you step-by-step instructions for changing who you are or where you are in life. Instead, this book will provide insight into how you became the person you are today and present you with ideas to help you create a genuine, meaningful life. Just as artists carefully consider each brush stroke that adds to the overall composition of their paintings, we can learn to pay close attention to specific experiences and choices that shape our identities. By the end of this book, you will better understand how your past experiences led you to where you are now and how you can chart a new, meaningful life for yourself and assist others in doing the same.

Your life is yours to design! The question now is: who do you want to be, and where do you want to go from here? I believe you'll find the answers in the pages of this book.

Part 1

IDENTIFYING THE UNDETECTED INFLUENCES; LAYING THE GROUNDWORK.

1

Showing What You're Made Of

Naughty by Nature or Nurture that's Naughty

Throughout the years, I've coached people who have repeatedly made the same mistakes, causing themselves great emotional pain and making a mess of their lives. Often, after much agony and introspection, the person would ask, "Why am I this way?" I'm sure we've all known someone who has been in this situation, or maybe you're here now. This question is profound if it is accompanied by deep self-reflection rather than a knee-jerk question of despair.

Our current thoughts, emotions, decisions, and experiences do not occur in a vacuum; they are all products of the past. A basic understanding of our past can help us better navigate the present and thrive in the future.

In other words, if we understand how genetic, environmental, and social influences affect our quality of life, we can capitalize on the positive and improve the negative. I believe diagnosing our past is key to designing our future. When we thoroughly consider the past influences on our lives, we can carefully plan new influences to shape who we become.

> **If we understand how genetic, environmental, and social influences affect our quality of life, we can capitalize on the positive and improve the negative.**

In the mid-nineteenth century, Francis Galton coined the phrase "nature versus nurture" to discuss how genes and the environment influence social progress.[1] Since then, modern psychologists have continued these studies in relation to human development. The question of whether we are products of our genetic inheritance or our environment has been heavily debated. In terms of an either/or dichotomy, I never understood why the two were pitted against each other. I remember researching this topic when I was a young philosopher before I got deeply entrenched in psychology. I suspected that nature and nurture could coexist and that we were missing a third category in the debate, which I call *nimble*. Hence, *nature*, *nurture*, and *nimble*. But more on that topic later.

Are we born with predetermined traits that shape who we are, or do our environmental experiences play a role? This question has perplexed philosophers and scientists for centuries, but the scientific study of twins may hold the answer to the role of genetic and environmental influences on personality. Identical twins share 100% of each other's DNA, while fraternal twins share 50%. Even when they are not raised together, evidence suggests that identical twins are far more similar in their personalities than fraternal twins. It is worth noting, however, that identical twins who are raised together are even more similar than identical twins who are not.[2] These findings suggest that, in addition to heredity, environment has a significant impact on personality. But we shouldn't assume that twins are psychologically identical and have no differences.

A Memoir by Two Identical Strangers

Elyse Schein and Paula Bernstein were identical twins adopted into different families soon after their birth in 1968. Paula grew up in a comfortable suburban family in New York. She loved her adoptive parents and older brother. Elyse also had a pleasant childhood, followed by college and film school overseas.

In 2003, Elyse inquired about her birth family at an adoption agency 35 years after she was adopted. According to the agency, she was the younger of twin sisters, and her twin, Paula, was looking for her. Elyse was moved to tears when she heard the news.

After calling Paula, Elyse felt like she heard her voice speaking back to her. The twins instantly connected, though they had never met and didn't know each other. The two met for lunch at a cafe and talked late into the night. I can imagine there would be a lot of catching up to do after 35 years. With the revelation of each new detail, the twins discovered astonishing similarities. They both studied film at graduate school. In addition, the two of them enjoyed writing, were editors of their high school newspapers, and had similar musical tastes.

Even though they shared many similarities, they also had unique life experiences. Elyse lost her adoptive mother and several close relatives. Despite all the twin studies on genetics, Elyse claimed that her environment forced her to develop stronger resilience, which Paula did not experience. As a result, Elyse couldn't imagine Paula confronting a tragedy such as the death of a close family member.[3] The twins now reside in Brooklyn and have collaborated on a book, *Identical Strangers*, recounting their childhood memories and the discovery of each other in their mid-thirties.

The Elyse and Paula twin study suggests that in addition to genetics, environment and experience play a significant role in shaping our personalities. Elyse developed psychological resilience in the face of loss, which Paula did not. Perhaps our genes provide a solid sketch, and our environmental experiences color in the details. The story of Elyse and Paula confirms what I believed as a young philosopher and what modern psychological research now shows: people are products of both nature and nurture.

Genetics Run Deep

Though scientists cannot pinpoint exactly how much hereditary and environmental factors each contribute to human development, genetics play a significant role in our lives. My friend Louis and his story highlight the value of genetic influence. At age 40, Louis discovered his biological father. However, he believed Marco, who raised him, was his biological father for forty years and even tattooed Marco's birthday on his arm. The relationship between Louis and Marco had always been tense due to their vastly different interests and perspectives. In addition, Louis despised how Marco treated his mother, causing a rift that prevented them from communicating for many years.

When Louis informed his mother, who was then divorced from Marco that he was considering recontacting him, his mother asked, "Son, what if he's not your father?" Louis was confused by his mother's response, and without any additional information, he dismissed it as his mother acting ridiculously. The following year, Louis informed his mother once more that he was considering contacting Marco, to which she responded, "What if Marco is not your father?" Upon hearing it a second time, Louis believed there was more to the statement. As a result, Louis took a DNA test on Ancestry.com, which revealed no biological connection between him and Marco. Instead, Louis shared DNA with a man named Javier, with precisely 3,475 centimorgans (cM), which is the highest match on Ancestry.com. Due to their resemblance in appearance, personality, and mannerisms, Louis' mother later admitted that she thought Javier was his biological father.

This information triggered an emotional tailspin in Louis, fueling his anger toward his mother. A short time later, Louis contacted Javier to disclose the news, which Javier had also suspected. Soon after, Javier flew to Charlotte, North Carolina, to meet his son, an experience Louis describes as meaningful and unforgettable. This union has brought Louis joy, and he and Javier talk often. Since then, Louis has met additional family members, including his half-brother. Louis says he is a lot like his biological father, and they share similar interests, perspectives, and personality traits. Interestingly, when I asked Louis what traits he acquired from his stepfather, Marco, that were different from those of his biological father, he said he is "quick-tempered." He feels this is an attribute he learned from interacting with his stepfather because neither his mother nor biological father have a short temper.

Many things that previously did not make sense to Louis now make sense. For example, before discovering his biological father, he recalls a time he worked at a bank and a man spoke Spanish to him. Because Louis didn't speak Spanish, the gentleman turned to a translator and asked if he was ashamed of his Hispanic heritage, to which Louis replied that he was full Italian. A few years later, Louis learned his biological father is of Hispanic descent, making him half-Italian and half-Hispanic.

Louis' story demonstrates the influence of genetics on who we are, yet I find it intriguing that we can develop characteristics that are not part of our genetic makeup. Nevertheless, there is always the possibility that certain genetic traits are dormant and waiting for the right environment and circumstances to awaken them.

Genes Set the Stage, Not the Show's Finale

We must gain an understanding of our genetic predispositions. To illustrate, my wife recently experienced a health scare from uncontrollable migraines and pain behind her right eye. After several doctor visits, the condition landed her in the hospital for three days, where she was diagnosed with optic neuritis. She underwent various tests and screenings to determine her likelihood of multiple sclerosis. All the doctors we consulted asked about her genetic history. There is no doubt that biological genes are passed from generation to generation. However, genes affect us not only physiologically but also psychologically. Personality traits and psychological disorders can all be linked to our genes. Our psychological characteristics are influenced by our brain, which is a physical organ affected by our genes, just like our eyes, heart, or height. There is even evidence that genetics can influence social and political attitudes, although to a lesser extent than personality and mental illness.[4]

It turns out our environment can influence our genes. Specific genes, for instance, can turn "on" and "off" when hormones are influenced by environmental conditions such as stress, loneliness, exercise, nutrition, obesity, sleep, etc. Success gurus tell us there will be time to "sleep when we die," a catchphrase for the "hustle" and "grind" pursuit of the American dream. In the same way that stress damages DNA, sleep deprivation affects how genes are expressed, leading to increased inflammation and damage to proteins that keep our bodies functioning. Perhaps one can get rich and die trying (to the rapper 50 Cent, no disrespect).

In addition to personality and social psychology, one of the college courses I have the privilege of teaching is developmental psychology. One semester, after covering the topic of *genetic expression*, I received several thank-you emails from my students who were particularly interested in the information presented by Nobel Prize winner Elizabeth Blackburn and health psychologist Elissa Epel. Their research shows that the process of aging can be sped up, slowed down, or even reversed. Through our actions, we can stop our telomeres (pronounced *tee-lo-meres*), an important part of the DNA in our cells, from getting shorter. Short telomeres are one of the primary causes of human cell aging, such as looking and feeling older. Many things contribute to telomere wear and tear, including cynical hostility, pessimism, rumination, thought suppression, negative thoughts, smoking, lack of physical activity, obesity, and pollution, resulting in premature aging.[5] Keep in mind that this is not an exhaustive list.

However, your telomeres carry out more than just the commands given to them by your genetic code. Telomeres are sensitive to things around you, such as diet, physical activity, psychological and emotional states, and how you react to challenges. One of the keys to good health is promoting healthy cell renewal through adequate sleep, proper nutrition, exercise, optimism, good environmental conditions, and avoiding chronic stress, to name a few contributors. You and I are born with a specific set of genes, but how we live can affect how our genes express themselves. As obesity researcher George Bray puts it, genes load the gun, but the environment pulls the trigger.[6]

> **You and I are born with a specific set of genes, but how we live can affect how our genes express themselves.**

These ideas put an end to the debate—both nature and nurture shape us. The human experience is a multifaceted phenomenon that involves the interaction of biology and our environment. Human genetics provide a framework on which environmental factors can act. Environmental influences, such as family relationships, cultural values, societal norms, and personal experiences, profoundly impact the development of people's identities, attitudes, and behaviors.

Apples Don't Fall Far from Trees

It's interesting to note that bias can impact our perception of genetic factors. For example, when we have positive qualities like intelligence or athleticism, people tend to attribute them to their genes and feel proud. However, when it comes to negative traits like addiction or mental illness, we often try to push the blame onto external factors and do not acknowledge the role of genetics. I sometimes see this imbalanced credit play out in my life. For instance, I always find it humorous when my dad says, "The apple doesn't fall far from the tree." His comments are usually in response to compliments about my personal characteristics, speaking abilities, or my positive work. Interestingly, my brothers have faced criminal charges, and my father has never said, "The apples don't fall far from the tree." (You should see my silent smirk.) We all have a *self-serving bias* that leads us to take credit for personal success and to blame our failures on external factors. However, both good and bad characteristics may be in the "apples" that don't fall far from the tree. Both hereditary and environmental factors can contribute to personality outcomes.

Among other things, my grandfather was a musician and public speaker. Growing up, I watched him sing and command audiences' attention and noticed how it energized him. Personality theorists might conclude that my grandfather was an extravert due to his outgoing and social nature. I also watched my father perform music and sing with my grandfather's band as a child. Eventually, he pursued public speaking and became a pastor. I am convinced that my father is also an extravert. Did he develop this characteristic through the grooming of his father, or is it an inherited trait? Despite being one of four brothers trained as musicians by my grandfather, my father is the only extravert and public speaker among them. Keep in mind that my grandmother was also a part of their genetic pool and an introvert.

Musical ability can be learned, whereas extraversion is a trait that may be developed within genetic boundaries. Perhaps my father and his brothers learned musicianship from my grandfather. Still, my dad was the only sibling who possessed a high degree of extraversion, which played a role in his decision to become a public speaker. It is important to note that not all speakers are extraverts, and not all extraverts are speakers: like musicianship, speaking (communication) is a learned skill. However, studies show introverts prefer writing rather than talking in public, working alone rather than in groups, and dislike being the center of attention, making them hesitant to speak in front of large crowds. Conversely, extraverts are sociable, energetic, chatty, and seek opportunities to engage with others, preferably in person. So, unlike introverts, extraverts prefer to talk to people rather than write—this is not to say that introverts cannot enjoy social interactions. Furthermore, it's also worth noting that these personality differences don't involve how well people speak in public—just how much they like to speak.[7]

Like my grandfather and father, I have a musical background, am highly extraverted, and am a public speaker. The major personality traits, extraversion, agreeableness, openness, conscientiousness, and neuroticism, all have a moderate amount of genetic influence. Genes, for example, account for roughly half of extraversion. As a result, I likely inherited a tendency toward extraversion from my grandfather and father. But this trait may have manifested in public speaking because of my environment (I watched my grandfather and father do it). So, in this case, the apple may not have fallen far from the tree. But remember, there are two trees—maternal and paternal. Even though my mother is not outgoing, I may have inherited other qualities from her, such as conscientiousness and agreeableness. I suspect that my social environment has also influenced these characteristics over the years.

My father also exhibits impulsivity, which refers to reacting quickly without conscious thought and results in low conscientiousness. People with impulsive characteristics have difficulty controlling their actions when presented with attractive goals or rewards. I don't appear to possess this trait, whereas my older and younger brothers do. In light of genetic expression theories, I may not have encountered or cultivated environments where the trait of impulsivity got "turned on;" therefore, I need to be careful not to stand on a personality pedestal. However, some evidence suggests that people differ as expressed by two biological systems in the brain. First, the *behavioral activation system (BAS)* directs or initiates behavior when it recognizes signs of rewards and incentives. The second system, the *behavioral inhibition system (BIS)*, stops or avoids behavior when it gets signals about punishment, frustration, or uncertainty. Comparing behavior to a car, the BAS is like the accelerator, and the BIS is like the brakes. Studies suggest that people differ in sensitivity in their BAS or BIS systems.[8] Individuals with impulsive tendencies are more likely to initiate (BAS) rather than avoid behaviors (BIS) and are less able to stop when there is a perceived reward.

Unfortunately, my father and brothers have had many problems over the years due to their impulsive behaviors. On the other hand, I haven't dealt with the issues they've faced, possibly because I may lean toward the BIS system, a trait that reflects my mother's personality. As a result, I may have been able to avoid trouble-causing situations more easily. Remember that although we all desire to take credit for good events and blame factors beyond our control for bad ones, "apples" do not fall according to a self-serving standard. My brothers possess other wonderful qualities, but impulsivity is also a part of the "apple" that hasn't fallen far from the tree.

We have all observed favorable and unfavorable characteristics in our parents. I am not ashamed that my parents possess characteristics I admire and dislike. Before we boast, our children will also grow up seeing things that they like and dislike in us. Nevertheless, my personal goal is to ensure that the good significantly outweighs the bad.

When I think about parent characteristics, I'm reminded of the story of Mylah, whose biological father passed away when she was an infant. She grew up with a loving stepfather whom she adored, although her parents divorced when she was 11. Mylah often saw her mother as angry and unhappy and believed she brought on many of her problems due to her irresponsibility, impatience, and lack of motivation. Puzzled by how different she was from her mother, Mylah vowed never to become like her. Instead, Mylah aspired to be like her stepfather, who she thought was optimistic, gentle, happy, and someone she could always count on for love and support.

Although Mylah lived in New York with her mother, she communicated almost daily via video chat and telephone with her stepfather, who lived in Los Angeles. In addition, she visited him during extended school breaks and holidays and enjoyed hearing about his work as an art therapist. The happiness he brought to others influenced her to follow in his footsteps. To be closer to him, she committed to attending college in Los Angeles after graduating high school. Instead of succumbing to hereditary or environmental influences caused by her mother, Mylah decided to try to become like her stepfather and change her surroundings. The choice was hers! Though an apple doesn't fall far from the tree, an external factor may carry it further away.

Jack Be Nimble

As we began this chapter, we learned that many people wonder why they are the way they are, and we have seen that people are influenced by their genetics and environment. However, as people learn more about

People can creatively arrange hereditary and environmental factors to construct who they desire to be and design a meaningful life.

these influences, they can decide to organize their lives and surroundings to improve themselves and their quality of life. This understanding leads me to my concept of *nimble*. As I previously stated, the nature-nurture framework is incomplete. By understanding what has made them who they are, people can creatively arrange hereditary and environmental factors to construct who they desire to be and design a meaningful life. This ability is what I call *nimble*. As Mylah perfectly demonstrates, she chose to adopt the traits of her *nonbiological* stepfather rather than her mother's characteristics, and she changed her environment. She was nimble!

Allow me to demonstrate how the desire for nimbleness affected my own life. I'm stubbornly flexible, and generally, I'm not too fond of rules. I've never been one to follow a crowd or jump on the latest trends or bandwagons. In most cases, I question why things are done the way they are and whether another way might be better. I don't like feeling boxed in or without options. And I don't give up easily. However, my anti-rigidity is within reason; I do not support lawlessness or anything that jeopardizes the safety and dignity of others. That said, it's no surprise that I kick against the walls of nature and nurture, searching for a "nimble" ceiling to break through. (Don't box me in, bro!)

I could summarize this book in one word: *Nimble*. The things we do and the things others do significantly influence our lives. Yet, because most people navigate their daily activities unconsciously, they are shaped more by their genetics and environment than by their conscious efforts. But by becoming aware of our daily routines, we can take action to address the mindless processes that shape who we are. Keep in mind that a person with lopsided priorities may lack the attention and discipline to follow through; you must care enough about your life to take action. Think of me as your coach as you move forward: in the following pages, I'll tell you what I'd say if we were talking one-on-one. Come on, let's move on to the next chapter and discover how your life story has shaped you today.

Chapter One Reflection Questions

1. Can you pinpoint and describe some of the inherited psychological and physical characteristics that may have shaped who you are today?

2. What role has your environment played in your life? Did it turn on or off certain genetic traits or influence other characteristics that have shaped who you are?

2

The Stories We Tell Ourselves

The Story of The Prince

Solomon King grew up in Africa in a small honor culture. His ability to connect with people and his knowledge of psychology and natural healing earned him respect. The community would yell, "King, King, King," whenever he visited town. Solomon had a son, and whenever his son got into trouble, Solomon would look him in the eyes and say, "You are Prince, you are Prince." Whenever the young boy encountered a problematic situation, Solomon would say, "You are Prince, you are Prince." And when the young boy needed encouragement, Solomon would say, "You are Prince, you are Prince."

As the boy grew older, he wondered what this meant, so he studied the ways of a prince. He'd practice his posture in the mirror and observe how his father interacted with the people in the community as they yelled, "King, King, King."

So, he imitated everything he saw and convinced himself he was a prince.

Solomon and his family later relocated to the United States. The young boy wanted to know how he was supposed to act in America, so he watched *the Fresh Prince of Bel-Air* and the movie *Coming to America*. However, when he went to public school, he noticed that the kids treated him differently, sometimes even poorly. As a result, he asked his father, "Dad, why don't American kids treat me like African kids do, as the prince I am." Solomon smiled and said, "No, no, no, I never said you are a prince; I said you're Prince, your name is Prince."

Though the *Story of Prince* is the type of story you might see in a Hollywood film, we can glean some truth from it. First, Solomon King seemed to understand the power of self-awareness. As he reminded his son of who he was, his statements contained implicit values and standards that shaped Prince's identity. People who learn to pay healthy attention to themselves become concerned with self-evaluation and how their current behaviors correspond to their own standards and beliefs. Because Prince paid so much attention to his father, he probably learned character traits and values that shaped his behavior. Second, Mr. King recognized the power and influence of prosocial behavior and treated others well, especially in front of his son. Through social influence, people affect each other in many ways, such as changing attitudes, beliefs, feelings, and behaviors. After seeing how influential and well-respected his father was, Prince modeled his attitudes and behavior after him. Due to all these factors, Prince began to adopt the characteristics associated with his name; he started telling himself a story about who he was.

> **Our stories define us because we live them as we tell them.**

Before we jump too far on the critical bandwagon and blame Solomon for allegedly misleading his son, most of us used to believe in the tooth fairy and Santa

Claus because of our parents, and neither of those beliefs resulted in the development of personal characteristics that Prince may have acquired. I would argue that the positive far outweighed the negative. The truth is that we all tell ourselves stories about who we are, our abilities, skills, and personal characteristics. Our stories define us because we live them as we tell them. Therefore, we should ask ourselves how these stories are shaping us.

The Narratives We Live By

Over the past two decades, personality theorists have become increasingly interested in autobiographical accounts, life stories, and narrative approaches to understanding human behavior. A growing interest in qualitative research methods and a better understanding of how people construct their own stories have motivated these approaches. Research in this area focuses on how people derive meaning from their experiences and develop their identities through telling themselves "stories" about their lives. Using narrative techniques such as metaphors, analogies, and themes, we reflect on and evaluate ourselves. As a result, the study of narrative psychology gives us valuable insights into why we think, feel, and behave the way we do, expanding our understanding of human personality.[9]

Narrative identity is the internalized and evolving story we create to explain how we came to be who we are today, an identity that furnishes purpose and meaning and a sense of unity within ourselves. Beginning in adolescence, we weave our reconstructed past, perceived present, and anticipated future into an identity that illustrates how we interpret our lives.[10] Thus, I agree with psychologists Howard Friedman and Miriam Schustack, who wrote that "the stories we tell ourselves—the narratives we live by—are crucial to the kind of persons we become."[11]

Creating a story is like constructing a building. We must choose the proper materials for our foundation, build upon it in stages, and ensure that everything fits together in the end.

Human life is a story with settings, scenes, characters, plots, and themes that show how people act on their desires, beliefs, and goals over time in different social settings.[9] Throughout history, storytelling has communicated profound truths about the human condition. As a result of social relationships and culture, these stories are constantly being created and re-created.[12]

Often, themes and images from a person's earliest years shape their adult life stories. Although children do not consciously create their identities by telling themselves integrated life stories that give their lives meaning and a sense of place in the world, they still gather information that will serve as the foundation for their future identities. This point perfectly illustrates a portion of my story. The first theme that emerged in my adult life story was influenced by my being held back in third grade and my teacher's second attempt to fail me. This foundational event led me to the conclusion that I was not smart, a notion that seemed to be confirmed by my teachers and peers. Once a narrative about our past is formed, we feel compelled to stick to this self-defining story because we believe it's true.[13]

Because I believed I was intellectually disadvantaged, my goal throughout my middle and high school years was just to get through. I was thrilled with just an average grade; I celebrated a C as if it were an A. In retrospect, I dealt with the dissonance of such thoughts by rationalizing that, while I lacked intellectual abilities, I possessed superior physical abilities that allowed me to excel in sports, particularly football. Despite my perceived lack, I saw myself as a ladies' man with swag and confidence. *Self-affirmation theory* underscores this point: we reduce dissonance and threats to our self-esteem by focusing on and affirming our competencies in unrelated areas.[14]

It's worth noting that while I was telling myself a negative story, I was also telling myself a story that I thought was positive but was not. As "the ladies' man," I adopted the narratives of popular music and films that emphasized the "player" mindset. (We'll get into meta-narratives in more detail short-ly). Furthermore, my peers highlighted, confirmed, and praised these characteristics. We all verify our existing beliefs by creat-ing a self-confirming social environment. (I'll discuss this more in the next chapter).

Getting back to my point, my primary purpose in enroll-ing in college after graduating high school was to escape my environment. Since I never truly believed I could graduate, I eventually dropped out of college and worked in several cor-porate entry-level positions. One day, I had a lengthy conver-sation with someone at work about God and the nature of the universe, to which he suggested that I should have pursued a degree in philosophy. His statement perplexed me because I thought philosophy was for smart people, and I believed I wasn't that smart. However, this gentleman thought I was in-telligent enough to study philosophy. I felt a glimmer of hope and wondered if he was right; had I defined myself for years based on inaccurate perceptions? That single interaction led me to tell myself a different story about my intelligence. Later, I studied philosophy as an undergraduate and graduate student, ultimately leading me to study psychology. My identity was undoubtedly determined by the stories I told myself. And, for better or for worse, you are doing the same thing.

The Existential Meta-narrative

Several years ago, I recalled watching my brothers hanging out and listening to music via a prerecorded video. It was the first time I felt they were doing more than just listening but ap-plying it deeply to their lives. It was as if I was watching a movie featuring the brothers I grew up with; they mimicked the song's words with their actions and demeanor, as if the rap artist was telling *their* personal story. Psychologically, they were taking on the story the artist gave them.

"Trap" music originated from the Southern United States, specifically Atlanta, where the word "trap" described houses used exclusively for selling drugs. Trap music paved the way for many artists, building careers worth millions of dollars, allowing them to leave "the trap" and lead legally successful lives. Although some have benefited by telling their "trap" stories within a redeeming narrative, others have not. The "trap" life leaves many more people dead or incarcerated. Ironically, several months after watching my brothers act out that video, they were both arrested for an alleged drug trafficking conspiracy by a joint drug task force comprised of the FBI and U.S. Marshals. My brothers now admit that they both created their narratives within another narrative. In other words, their stories were influenced by the trap artists' stories.

Interestingly, we all tend to create a story within a story. For example, when I was 15, my older brother (whom I just discussed) was sent to prison for 2nd-degree murder. Consequently, I spent most of my teenage years in the streets; I grew up quickly and carried a gun to emulate my older brother. He would often call me from prison, telling me not to come in there, or I would wish I were dead. For years, I heard his statement like loud echoes in my ears.

In my late high school years, I began to feel like I was put on earth for a reason. As I grew spiritually, I became more aware of how some of the music I listened to influenced me. Even though I loved the music, I felt a deep need to take a break. My story was being influenced and shaped by the stories the rappers told, and I knew it. Stories have the power to both affirm and confirm aspects of our lives. Generally, affirming something means stating it positively, whereas confirming a thing determines its accuracy. In affirming and confirming ways, stories influence who we are and how we see ourselves.

Many music artists create their identities through stage names and the stories they tell. It's a form of self-expression and influences how others perceive them. No doubt, the roles that artists take on and the messages they wish to convey in their songs are closely linked to who they are (or were). Pseudonyms such as Snoop Dogg or Lady Gaga allow individuals to express themselves more freely and create a persona that audiences can relate to and appreciate. Typically, these stage names embody the artist's ideals and values, allowing them to present their identity in a unique way.

There is, however, a mutual influence between artists and the stories they tell. The artists create their stories, but their stories also influence them—much like two people playing catch with a ball. They both influence the direction and speed of the ball as it moves back and forth between them. In some ways, the ball represents identity. Like my brothers, many of us create narratives based on the narratives of musical artists. However, artists are not excluded; they also create narratives based on other narratives. Like every other aspect of identity, past, present, and future experiences play an essential role. An artist's identity is likely to be influenced by other artists as well as their own imagination. Like ordinary people, artists also become the stories they tell themselves, though a bit more creatively.

I believe that we are all subject to what I call the *existential meta-narrative*. In today's world, individuals invest years in different group settings, such as academic or job training, to master personal and professional life skills that arise from social expectations. And we use this knowledge to equip ourselves within a specific subculture or community. These social expectations, in turn, establish a cultural framework for our entire life story. As a result, we create our narrative identities based on or contrary to these prevailing worldviews. In this way, each person's life narrative is built on society's master narrative (template or script). Some people's storylines are exactly in keeping with societal norms, while the life stories of others take on a counter-narrative or a different shape because of it.

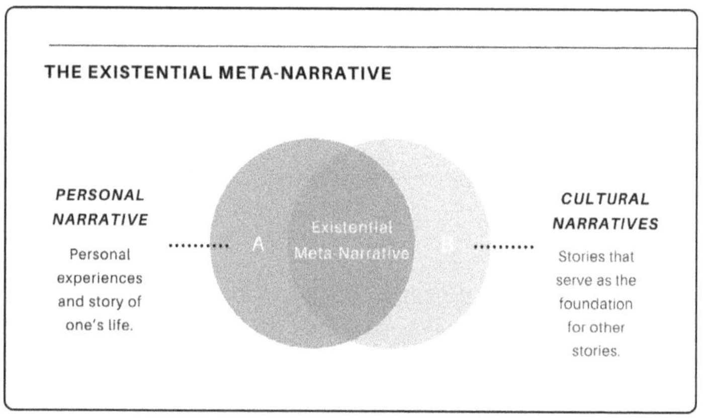

Figure 2.1 - The Existential Meta-Narrative

Behind the Psychological Scenes

After considering the narratives created by music performers, shifting our focus to the stories created by individuals within theater and film is appropriate. As *Cultivation Theory* suggests, regular exposure to television or mass media has a cumulative effect on our beliefs and attitudes, influencing our perception of reality. Although mass media includes much more than film, I'll focus on the acting industry here. A meta-narrative is relatively easy to recognize as we relate to television series or movies; however, it also works in the opposite direction, as many of these films are based on true stories (several of the points discussed in the previous section can also be applied here.) However, questions arise about the psychological implications when actors become immersed in their roles.

"Getting into character" is a complex phenomenon that requires more than just assuming or discarding a role. It requires mental and physical changes and a deep understanding of the character's personality traits, motivations, emotions, and physical mannerisms. Furthermore, a performer must develop an intimate knowledge of the values and behaviors associated with their particular character and surrounding environment—all to craft a believable, dynamic performance. Critical self-reflection ensures that the character's qualities are accurately portrayed. Even though the actor conforms to the script, the script also conforms to them; two stories blend into one.

Actors often alter their body weight and physical features to portray another person's experience better. For example, the movie "Ray Charles" tells the story of one of the most iconic soul musicians of all time, played by Jamie Foxx. To effectively tell Charles' story, it was essential to portray his loss of sight during childhood and how he adapted throughout his life and musical career. Foxx perfectly matched Charles' piano skills, voice, cadence, and mannerisms, but he still had to act the part as if he couldn't see. To do this, Foxx had his eyelids glued shut for 14 hours a day and agreed to wear prosthetic eyelids based on Charles' eyelids rather than opaque glasses.

In the first two weeks of filming, Foxx admitted to experiencing anxiety attacks while applying prosthetic eyelids. He also said there were several days when he wasn't sure what was happening to his mind and body. For the most realistic performance, Jamie Foxx had to learn how to adapt to his loss of sight, which required a lot of time, discomfort, and mental and physical energy. This example illustrates the depths to which actors will go to "get into character." But I'm curious if we "non-professional actors" aren't all that different, but more on that later.

For a moment, allow me to digress and discuss human attention. Our minds navigate the world using what psychologists call *selective attention*, which means that we see what we are looking for, and what we aren't looking for tends to go unnoticed. People selectively attend to particular things and ignore others. For example, if you and I were in a crowded coffee shop having a thought-provoking conversation, the chatter of other people would fade into the unconscious background—a phenomenon known as the *cocktail party effect*. If, however, a person mentioned one of our names in the noisy chatter, we'd both become aware of our surroundings and turn to look in the direction we heard our names. Our names are strong enough to cut through the incomprehensible cacophony of many people speaking at once.

A study published in the Journal of Cognitive Neuroscience showed that professional acting can significantly impact the basic mechanisms of the human brain. Wearable brain imaging technologies revealed that when actors heard their names during a performance, their response was suppressed in the left anterior prefrontal cortex, which is commonly associated with self-awareness. However, during non-acting times, the performers responded normally to hearing their names. Shouting a person's name, as in our earlier coffee shop example, activates the brain's prefrontal cortex and will usually prompt a response. Yet, studies suggest that when actors "get into character," they may learn to suppress their sense of self.[15]

In some cases, actors can become so engrossed in their characters that their identities become entwined. Getting "stuck in character" occurs when the actor profoundly adopts the character's traits. Upon finishing a role, actors generally return to their everyday lives, surrounded by family, relationships, and habits that keep them grounded; however, a character may be stickier than the actor imagines. When actors temporarily suppress their sense of self, changes in their brains can allow them to open the door to the narrative identities of their characters. Consequently, actors may unintentionally adopt their characters' qualities, beliefs, and values, making each character part of them.

Acting is a powerful art form, and those who become actors learn to navigate the power of storytelling. Performers often draw from personal experiences or elements from their lives that offer insight into how

It is critical for all of us, including professional actors, to examine our roles and determine whether they align with our personal convictions.

they view characters. Not only do they act out stories on stage or screen, but they also tell themselves stories to create their own personalities, as we all do. Each story an actor tells, whether work-related or personal, shapes their craft and contributes to the fabric of their identity. Every role an actor chooses not only reflects some aspect of who they are but also reveals something about their values and beliefs. It is critical for all of us, including professional actors, to examine our roles and determine whether they align with our personal convictions. Keep in mind that we all become immersed in our *social* roles. (I'll discuss roles a bit more in the following chapter).

I want to emphasize, however, that actors who portray villains are not inherently evil but do so for reasons that reflect their own values. Tom Hiddleston, for instance, plays villains in films to challenge himself as an actor and explore the complexity of human nature. Some may have a different motivation and find it appealing to take on the mischievous and nefarious to suppress their real-world pain or hatred, knowing that villains sometimes say exactly what the rest of us think—things that may not be socially acceptable. Regardless of the reason, actors take on roles and align them with their values in some way. To be true to themselves while fully inhabiting a role, actors must understand the type of story they wish to tell. This aspect makes acting so unique; it allows performers to create their own narratives as part of a shared experience with an audience.

Interestingly, we all "get into character," living and embodying different roles. William Shakespeare once said, "All the world's a stage," referring to the idea that we are all actors on the same stage performing different plays. We perform for various audiences, including family, friends, coworkers, strangers, and those on social media. Our daily lives can be seen as a sequence of performances where we face new challenges and roles in social settings. Every day, we carefully manage our impressions to influence others to see us the way we want to be seen. As individuals, we are not fixed in one role but have an array of characters that help us navigate daily life and unique situations. Like professional actors, our chosen characters can tell us a lot about ourselves if we take the time to analyze them properly.

An Epic Tug-of-War

Our internal dialogue heavily influences who we are and what roles we play in life. Our beliefs and emotions influence how we behave and interact with others. Analyzing our inner dialogue can help us understand why we take certain paths in our lives or why certain decisions and reactions appear rational to us. Each of us has an ongoing internal dialogue that shapes how we see ourselves and the world. Our inner monologue, or "self-talk," helps us understand ourselves and make sense of our environment. Our individual micro-narratives can be powerful motivators or cause significant obstacles in our lives. Have you ever noticed how one negative thought can lead to another? Similarly, positive thoughts can inspire more positive thoughts. But our thoughts about ourselves, others, and our environment, whether they be positive or negative, are not always based on reality.

Kurt Lewin, known as the father of social psychology, relied on the Gestalt school of thought, stressing that studying how people perceive something in their minds is more important than looking at how it *actually* is. He believed that it was more meaningful to understand how people perceive, comprehend, and make sense of behavior than to examine its objective properties. Older schools of thought, such as *behaviorism*, overlook this point because they ignore the emotional and mental aspects of human interaction. To be meaningful, therapy must take into account how people construe their experiences.

Everyone interprets events, circumstances, and human behavior from their unique perspective, shaped by their experiences, genetic predispositions, and environment. If interpretations are incorrect, they can lead to *misperceptions*—mental representations that differ from reality or the objective facts of a situation. Misperceptions can include extreme views of oneself and others. Thinking overly negatively or too positively about ourselves or others can result in self-handicapping behaviors that hinder personal growth and cause us to overlook flaws and weaknesses, creating unrecognized blind spots.

Negative thinking habits can have a profound impact on our personalities. Engaging in constant negative self-talk reinforces negative beliefs about ourselves and the world around us. Over time, this can lead to a host of negative changes in our personalities, including increased anxiety, decreased self-esteem, and dispositional pessimism.

Extreme pessimists are their own worst critics because they focus too much on their own perceived flaws and weaknesses, which can cause them to lose hope and abandon their dreams. Furthermore, they tend to see the worst in other people and situations. As such, a negative cycle can impede growth and progress by exacerbating frustration and disappointment, affecting our perception of ourselves and our interactions with others.

My ideas on negative self-talk resonated with a young lady named Cora, who had always considered herself to be shy and self-conscious. Cora wanted to be a professional photographer and attended the University of North Carolina at Charlotte to study fine arts. However, her negative self-talk often undermined her confidence. As a first-generation college student, she frequently scolded herself whenever she faced a challenge, telling herself she was not talented or good enough. This way of thinking gradually harmed her relationships and decreased her motivation. Cora suffered silently as her inner voice condemned many of her actions. Every mistake was a reminder of why she shouldn't try, so eventually, Cora stopped.

Cora dropped out of college and returned to her hometown, which she called "the land of destitute dreams." She now works in a retail pet store, a job she despises and sees as punishment for failing to measure up. So, I suggested she take unique photos of the pets to capture their distinct personalities. In addition, I advised her to modify her negative self-talk using cognitive behavioral therapy strategies to identify thinking distortions, such as confusing a thought with a fact, jumping to conclusions, all-or-nothing thinking, negative filtering, catastrophizing, and personalizing events. If Cora takes these suggestions seriously, she can get back on track.

Negative self-talk has a detrimental impact on our motivation and relationships and can lead to anxiety, depression, and social isolation. Some people may be more susceptible to negative thoughts than others. *Neuroticism* is a personality trait that involves high levels of anxiety, anger, depression, and other negative emotions. People who score high in neuroticism are often overly sensitive, worrying excessively about their actions or the opinions of others. They also often overthink situations and can become overwhelmed with negative emotions.

Those who are high in neuroticism easily contaminate their personal stories by interpreting their experiences as rapidly changing from good to bad. For instance, a man may tell a story about the success of his daughter's brain surgery, which is a joyful moment, but then immediately conclude with the death of his brother, who passed away a couple of years later. The tragic event tarnishes the daughter's success story. Individuals whose personalities are predisposed to neuroticism quickly incorporate a negative turn of events into their conversations without even realizing it.

Genetic factors – including an overactive (BIS) behavioral inhibition system that we discussed earlier—may contribute to neuroticism. Still, stressful life events such as job loss, divorce, or the death of a loved one may exacerbate it. Additionally, neuroticism may result from low self-esteem, being overly critical of oneself, or feeling insecure in new environments. People high in neuroticism must recognize their strengths and weaknesses and intentionally cultivate healthy coping strategies like mindfulness practices, exercise, connecting with friends and family, or seeking professional help if necessary.

Although mental health professionals encourage the practice of positive self-talk to boost motivation and improve self-esteem, there are times when we are too optimistic about ourselves. This attitude is particularly applicable in situations involving narcissistic behaviors. A narcissistic person demonstrates excessive self-love and little empathy for others. Due to their inflated yet fragile self-esteem, narcissists may become blind to the consequences of their actions and believe they are superior to others. Meanwhile, someone with moderate narcissism may tell themselves only positive stories to avoid confronting unpleasant truths about themselves or their lives. In any case, narcissism manifests as an exaggerated sense of self-worth and grandiose thinking.

In Greek mythology, *Narcissus* illustrates the dangers of thinking too highly of oneself. One version of the story conveys a prophet telling his mother that *Narcissus* would live a long life if he never knew himself. As the story goes, as the handsome boy grew older, he never met anyone who could make him fall in love. As a result, he left many young ladies brokenhearted. Then, one day, he saw himself in a pool of water and fell in love with the image reflected back to him. This one-sided obsession inevitably failed. Sadly, *Narcissus* could not pull himself away from his reflection in the water, where he wallowed in despair until he died of thirst and starvation.[17]

The story of *Narcissus* has been a cautionary tale for centuries. However, the same self-obsession permeates social media, where selfies (reflections) and other images highlighting the positive images of oneself dominate the digital pool. Many individuals are addicted to perfecting their presence online and creating an idealized version of themselves that may not exist in reality; they spend countless hours perfecting their portraits, not only to impress others but also to satisfy their own scrutiny.

Such attention-seeking practices lead people to devote a great deal of time to analyzing the likes, shares, and comments made. Some waste countless years staring into the social media pool and fail to reach their full potential. In many ways, *Narcissus'* actions aren't much different from those on social media today.

Like negative self-talk, thinking too positively has similar drawbacks and can lead us down a potentially dangerous path when combined with low awareness of our weaknesses or blind spots—failure to acknowledge our mistakes or areas where improvement is needed stunts our learning and personal growth. In general, the key is to find a balance between negative and positive self-talk and not veer too far in one direction or the other. Rather than high self-esteem, we should strive for optimal self-esteem, which includes having accurate views of ourselves, whether positive or negative, as this can increase our self-awareness and allow us to improve. Folks who set themselves up on pedestals may have unrealistic expectations of themselves. As with negative self-talk, one may become discouraged or frustrated when one fails to meet those standards, resulting in further negative emotions like depression or guilt.

> **Rather than high self-esteem, we should strive for optimal self-esteem, which includes having accurate views of ourselves.**

A Thousand Words

To conduct an honest quality check on our lives, we must find a way to step outside of ourselves and, as neutral observers, evaluate our prior narratives—this is an aspect of mindfulness that I admire. To complement this approach, I'd like to suggest a "narrative audit," which is analyzing past episodic content to identify a personal narrative theme and evaluate its merits and value (I'll discuss narrative audits in more detail in Chapter 4.) To unpack this a bit, we can think of episodic memory as a place where our life's events and experiences are stored. Episodic memory content may include, among other things, smells, places, past homes, movies, music, and photos, which can jog memories of our past experiences.

While wrapping up this chapter, I came across some old photographs. We've all heard the expression, "A picture is worth a thousand words." Interestingly, every image I discovered gave me "a thousand words" (equivalent to a three-page essay) and revealed powerful things about who I was then. I could see my own evolution as well as the accompanying narratives. As I looked through all the photos from different seasons of my life, I didn't like most of the stories they told me. Some images showed stories of arrogance, superficial pursuits, a bad-boy manner, attention-seeking, and an aura of being the life of the party. Thousands of words ensued, and even though each experience shaped me, my stories weren't always helpful. However, I appreciated the photos that captured the beginnings of who I am today: someone dedicated to helping others live better lives.

What might you discover if you did a "narrative audit" of old and recent photos? Similar stories to mine, such as negative self-talk or overly positive self-thoughts mixed with superficial pursuits and meaningless experiences? Or would you see evidence of your transformational journey? Hopefully, you have learned by now that we are all creating and writing our life stories as we go. According to psychologists Dan McAdams and William Dunlop, "The most important story we ever tell is the story of our lives."[15] It's worth noting that the stories we tell don't solely originate within ourselves because we also see ourselves through the eyes of others. Since other people significantly impact who we become, we must understand how others influence us. The study of social psychology has much to say about how people are influenced by others. So, join me as we embark on this next chapter and discover how others help shape who we are today.

Chapter Two Reflection Questions

1. Describe some stories that have shaped your narrative identity. What stories are you telling about yourself now that others can easily recognize?

2. Summarize how your constructed narratives have benefited or harmed your life, focusing on personal development, relationships, and fulfillment. (Include any excessively negative or positive self-talk).

$$3$$

Your Circle Matters

To Belong or Not to Belong

I grew up in a time that was not as racially and socially progressive as it is today. My younger brother and I attended an all-white elementary school in the 1980s. Despite our best efforts to fit in, we were reminded every day of our differences. Although we had some white friends and even a couple of girlfriends (puppy love), I still recall my search for a sense of belonging and acceptance. As a child, I felt insecure and uncomfortable, especially during social events at school. I couldn't help but compare myself to my lighter-skinned friends and classmates, who seemed more socially accepted within our school community. To make matters worse, the physical characteristics of the students matched those of the white teachers.

As early as preschool, we naturally divide people into groups and evaluate ourselves by the groups we belong to. Labeling and categorizing things are an integral part of human nature. Humans classify other people like biologists classify plants and animals; our brains are hardwired to categorize, organize, and simplify our surroundings. As a result, it isn't surprising that we tend to group people together based on social identity traits, such as race, gender, and religion. This urge to classify people by social traits is a powerful force, allowing us to make sense of the world around us.

The sense of being different from others in one's current environment, which reflected the attitudes my brother and I shared, is known as *solo status*. We never quite fit in and found establishing meaningful relationships with our peers difficult. Also, my mother was worried about how well my teacher cared for and helped me, so she moved us to a different school district when my third-grade teacher tried to hold me back for the second time.

Near the end of the school year and during my second attempt at third grade, we transferred to a racially integrated school. Something fundamentally changed inside me. Seeing students who looked like me in the classroom made me feel safer and more secure than ever before. For the first time in my life, I began to see myself in my peers. I found a sense of belonging, a feeling of camaraderie and understanding that was lacking before.

When we feel like we belong, we better understand who we are. Our identities are, in part, defined by our groups. Throughout our lives, we strive to understand our personal and social identities. *Personal identity* is a portrait of how we see ourselves based on our characteristics, life experiences, societal roles, relationships, abilities, etc. On the other hand, *social identity* refers to our group memberships and social categories, such as ethnicity, religion, political affiliations, occupation, or any other social group. Our social identities reflect how we perceive ourselves in social contexts, and this perception plays a crucial role in shaping our personal identities, as well as our attitudes and behaviors. Remember that our identity is fundamentally a narrative in which we create an internalized, ever-changing story about ourselves.

To return to my point, my brother and I both experienced positive changes to our self-esteem as we interacted with the kids in our new environment, which was reflected in our behavior. We were energized by the opportunity to develop friendships with other youngsters who shared our identity, primarily our ethnic background. And we felt a sense of pride in our shared experience with the other kids. According to developmental psychologists, children's friendships are typically defined by similarity. Throughout childhood, friends are more similar than dissimilar in age, ethnicity, and other factors.[18] By forming friendships with youths from similar backgrounds, my brother and I gained a better understanding of ourselves.

Through the Eyes of Others

Charles Cooley's concept of the "looking-glass self" helps us understand how our concept of self develops from how we think others perceive us. His famous quote, "I am not who you think I am; I am not who I think I am; I am who I think you think I am," precisely expresses his point of view. In other words, we adopt views of ourselves that reflect how we *think* others perceive us, which may or may not match how they *actually* see us. As a result, we use the perceived opinions of others to construct our identities, evaluate ourselves, and judge our actions. Cooley suggests people change their beliefs about themselves due to the perceptions of people they love and admire rather than the perceived views of strangers.[19]

> **We adopt views of ourselves that reflect how we think others perceive us, which may or may not match how they actually see us.**

This doesn't mean that strangers do not affect who we become. We all have *self-presentational* goals that influence how we present ourselves to others, including strangers; we want people to view us in particular ways.

The concept of the looking-glass self continues to affect us throughout adulthood, but it significantly impacted me during my earlier years. My brother and I believed our friends and neighbors viewed us more favorably after we transferred to our new school; as a result, our personalities developed based on the characteristics that we thought they perceived in us. For example, I was shy at the all-white school, likely due to insecurity about how I thought other kids perceived me. However, as I internalized my peers' perceptions of me and became more secure in my surroundings at my new school, I began to think of myself as more outgoing. In other words, my perception of myself changed from believing that I was introverted to extraverted because I felt that was how my new peers saw me.

We are all influenced by the "looking-glass self." However, those who are unfamiliar with sociology or psychology often object to Cooley's idea, as well as their proclivity to present themselves in ways that control how others perceive them. I recently spoke with a family member who stated that he didn't care what others thought of him, which is *completely* false. Whether we admit it or not, we are all influenced by the opinions of others, especially those close to us. I believe, in part, the objection is related to our cultural mantra to "be your authentic self." In fact, you may be wondering, "How can I be my true self if 'the self' is influenced by others?"

The first issue with becoming our "authentic self" is that we assume authenticity is always good. Sadly, people can have *authentically* bad characteristics. Perhaps public figures such as Donald Trump and Kanye West are being their authentic selves. Furthermore, people can be *authentically* evil, such as Jeffrey Dahmer, Adolf Hitler, and Elizabeth Báthory. To take it a step further, mass murderers, robbers and thieves, pedophiles, and human traffickers may act according to their beliefs about who they are. As a result, we would not want these individuals to "be their authentic selves" but to seek help instead.

The second issue is that "the self" is not static—it is flexible, complex, and ever-evolving. Because we are constantly changing, I am skeptical of the concept of an *authentic* self. We all intuitively customize and adjust aspects of our behavior in various social contexts to meet the demands of our environment. Moreover, our values, preferences, and beliefs also shift as we get older and have new experiences. Interestingly, the question, "Who am I?" is difficult to answer for many reasons: we are many things simultaneously, some of our characteristics may contradict each other, and we will certainly change over time. Whatever words we use to describe ourselves do not fully capture who we are.

I'm all for telling people to be themselves, but I'm not sure we entirely understand what that means. Each one of us has a propensity for both good and evil; being ourselves includes both. When it contributes to our flourishing and the well-being of others, we should be ourselves—that is, lean into our character strengths, values, and unique ways of expression. However, we should strive to *improve* (rather than *be*) ourselves in areas where our traits are detrimental to ourselves and others.

> **We should strive to improve (rather than be) ourselves in areas where our traits are detrimental to ourselves and others.**

To return to the topic, the groups we associate with throughout our lives serve as a mirror (a looking glass) through which we perceive and understand ourselves. Looking back on my life, I can see how various groups I have been a part of, for better or worse, have influenced me and made me who I am today. For example, in high school, my Casanova-like traits were heightened by my perceptions of how others viewed me. I thought I was cool and charming because I believed that everyone around me thought so. (In Chapter 5, I will discuss my groups' influence on me today.) Whether it is family or a peer group, an academic or collegiate group, or a work or community group that we join as we transition from childhood to adulthood, we extract information from individuals that we *think* tell us something about ourselves and use it to define and understand who we are.

A central focus of social psychology is emphasizing other people's influence on us. Interestingly, almost everything we do involves other people, whether they are physically present, imagined, or implied in some way. I believe the "looking-glass self" can also relate to how we *think* an imagined community perceives us. The concept of *imagined community* is consistent with the late political scientist and historian Benedict Anderson's work, describing a nation as a socially constructed community imagined by individuals—who see themselves as belonging to it. Back to my point, a person or group does not need to be physically present in our lives to influence who we are and the kind of person we become. I've noticed this phenomenon when observing the attitudes and behaviors of my brothers. Because they believe they are perceived as "real" on the streets (a sense of street credibility), they act in ways that reinforce these beliefs. Notice that the "streets" are not an actual group of people but an imagined or implied group.

Individuals from all walks of life experience the "looking-glass self" based on their perceptions of how they believe a hypothetical group would perceive them. Each of us may use an imaginary group as a feedback loop to inform our beliefs about ourselves and our attitudes and behaviors. To illustrate, "robe-itis" (or "black robe-itis") is used to describe judges who assume a god-like attitude and power, believing that their rulings are above reproach. Some judges are more likely to have these attitudes if they *think* that the culture of the court views them as god-like (once again, the culture of the court is an *imagined* community rather than an actual group of people.)

Robert A. Kessler expressed a similar concern in his article, *The Psychological Effects of the Judicial Robe*. Kessler recounts how a Florida judge, horrified by a fellow judge's misconduct, removed his robe and refused to wear it again until the bench was treated with dignity and respect.[20] In addition, Kessler stated, "The judge himself, of course, is not immune to the *aura* which surrounds the robe. He too believes in his divinity, and this tends to make him unwilling to accept changes in the law even when legislatively enacted."[20] Thus, a court's culture, in which judges are seen as infallible and omnipotent in their decisions, can reinforce an unhealthy sense of power. Consequently, simply identifying with a certain caste or group and one's beliefs about how they are perceived through the *implied* group's eyes is enough for the "looking-glass self" to take shape.

The Strength of the Crowd

Hopefully, you have started to understand how the presence of others and our beliefs about them can affect us positively and negatively. We intuitively understand that we are influenced by others, even if we are unaware of the specific psychological processes at work. We are all familiar with cultural idioms such as "birds of a feather flock together" and Bible verses like "bad company corrupts good character." These adages are evidence of our collective understanding of group influence. However, in addition to seeing ourselves through the eyes of others, we also use our groups to reinforce our current attitudes and behaviors. To demonstrate, I am often asked how I changed from who I was to who I am now. If I'm being honest, the unfolding of each chapter answers that question; however, I'll address it more specifically in Part Two of this book. Nevertheless, it is important to understand what kept me entangled with my old self, which is the same for everyone. As humans, we are inclined to seek out other people and situations that confirm how we see ourselves, known as *self-verification*. Our desire to be around people who affirm our existing beliefs about ourselves helps us gain clarity about our identity.

My peers and social environment confirmed my attitudes and behaviors as a teen. People who were like me frequently praised my bling-bling (the popular slang at the time), bad boy persona, and womanizing ways, encouraging me to continue these behaviors and see them as validating aspects of my identity. I also saw myself the same way; my peers and environment confirmed it. Their praise was like being awarded an unofficial badge of honor for maintaining that way of life. Unfortunately, this positive reinforcement pushed me further down that path, making it more challenging to break away or reconsider my actions. Being around teens who carried guns confirmed my idea to do so. In our community, the street mentality represented respect and fearlessness. As a result, we followed the example of older guys we admired, and the younger kids followed ours, creating an endless cycle. Our social environment was a self-confirming one that validated our views and thinking.

All people seek peer support and affirmation to validate their beliefs and identities. As a young student enthralled by philosophy, I was eager to learn. So, naturally, I immersed myself in this subject and hung around a community of philosophers and theologians with similar interests. Often, our dialogues about ancient and medieval philosophers, God, the nature of the Universe, morality, ethics, and the Bible became a form of social validation that helped us maintain consistent views of ourselves and our beliefs.

Self-verification occurs in many contexts, including gangs, fraternities, sororities, religious groups, book clubs, business groups, and sports teams, to name a few. For example, when someone joins a gang, they are surrounded by individuals who have had similar experiences or share the same ideals, providing them with the acceptance, belonging, and validation of new peers. Similarly, fraternities and sororities also offer the sense of a confirming community, focusing on academic and social camaraderie and shared values within the organization. Book clubs can use their platform to share personal stories about how the book resonated with them; typically, the group agrees, which boosts their confidence and creates a bond that may extend outside the group.

In any group, we strive to have our personal beliefs validated by our peers, which comes in the form of compliments or shared values. We may also find ourselves seeking approval from one another. Like my earlier groups, some peers may be detrimental to our flourishing. With this in mind, we are responsible for determining the benefits of peer groups and understanding how their feedback and our need for validation can influence us.

Another way groups influence us is that we often conform to their norms and values. For instance, we can demonstrate conformity in how we dress and talk, our views on religion and politics, social issues, and our behaviors. Perhaps the adage "monkey see, monkey do" holds some truth. As we observe the behavior of others in our group, we consciously and unconsciously start to mimic it. Our mimicry is partly due to our desire to maintain cohesiveness in our groups and to feel accepted and respected by our peers, which is a basic human need. Incvitably, the threat of being rejected by our groups undermines our need to belong. Simply put, we fear being excluded from our groups because belonging is essential to who we are.

The tendency to conform has been further reinforced by the fact that, since childhood, conformity has been rewarded, and going against the grain has been generally discouraged. In addition, social norms and expectations further reinforce conformity; they are our society's written and unwritten rules, which we feel compelled to follow to be accepted and maintain social harmony. Our conformity is an adaptation to changing environments, enabling us to create and maintain social order over generations. Although conforming is important to maintain an orderly society, it can sometimes lead to mistakes in the way we make decisions and behave.

During the writing of this chapter, I saw an interview with attorney Antonio Romanucci advocating for justice for Tyre Nichols, a 29-year-old black man who was beaten to death by five Memphis police officers. Nichols complained of shortness of breath during the incident and was transported by ambulance to a nearby hospital in critical condition. Sadly, a photo posted on social media showed him in the hospital, violently bruised and breathing through a tube. Three days after the incident, Nichols succumbed to his injuries.

According to the review, the officers violated several departmental policies, including the use of force, the duty to intervene, and the duty to render aid. As a result, the Memphis Police Department announced that all five officers had been fired. "The egregious nature of this incident is not a reflection of the good work that our officers perform with integrity every day," the Police Chief said.[21]

Due to the long history in America of racial tension between people of color and the police, you may have been surprised to learn that all the officers involved in the murder of Tyre Nichols were black. By applying a social psychological lens to this incident, two main themes can be identified: *conformity* and *deindividuation*. As discussed earlier, *conformity* is the act of altering beliefs, attitudes, or behaviors to align them with those of others.[19] Some of the officers most likely acted solely out of conformity. The troubling reality is that this conformity power can lead to the deaths of innocent people through unjustified police shootings, excessive force, beatings, and other incidents in which many officers fail to intervene. When surrounded by colleagues with rogue mindsets, police officers can lose sight of their values and conform to the group's standards, leading to poor decisions.

Many groups exhibit conformity, including friend groups, classmates, workplace environments, sports teams, political parties, committees, etc. Individuals in these groups may feel compelled to act or think in accordance with the group's decisions and norms. In the workplace, for instance, employees may find it difficult to challenge work-related decisions that go against their own personal beliefs if they fear alienation from colleagues and supervisors. Such conformity, which prioritizes group harmony and cohesion, is vulnerable to *groupthink*, in which members fail to address issues critically because of social pressures to reach a consensus.[19]

Regarding political groups, conformity can be dangerous as it can lead to the suppression of dissenting voices or even the complete exclusion of minority perspectives on essential matters. When this happens, decisions become biased toward one side, with little regard for those outside the dominant opinion.

To demonstrate these patterns, I assigned students in one of my social psychology courses to watch a news segment examining a political issue from opposing news broadcasts and identify the cognitive biases I had taught them. *Confirmation bias*, a tendency to favor things that confirm one's existing beliefs, was the most prevalent type of bias that emerged. Unsurprisingly, it is the mother of all biases because we tend to *believe first* and *then justify* rather than accept a justification that leads to belief.

> **We tend to *believe first* and *then justify* rather than accept a justification that leads to belief.**

Overall, conformity is reinforced by an individual's desire for social acceptance and a leader-follower power structure. As I binge-watched the latest episode of *Tom Clancy's Jack Ryan* series, I was inspired by the final statement made by Luka Gocharov (the character played by James Cosmo). He said, "There are no heroes in our profession. But occasionally, there are good men. *Men who act on what is right. Not simply doing what they are told.*"[22] Let us always remember to demonstrate this degree of social responsibility and conscientiousness to do the right thing for ourselves and others.

I Disappear When *We* Appear

Among the most significant aspects of group influence is its ability to reduce self-awareness as well as important characteristics about oneself. Social psychologists have been intrigued by this phenomenon for many decades, devoting countless research studies to understanding how this self-removal process occurs in groups. As such, *deindividuation* describes the experience of losing one's sense of individuality in the company of a group or crowd.[19] In other words, people temporarily lose self-awareness and become susceptible to the influences of the group or situation. People in a deindividuated state have a reduced ability to think clearly about their actions, so they may not monitor or control their behavior as usual.[23] You've probably heard someone say, "I just got lost in the crowd," after behaving foolishly. This statement has some truth; hence, *I* disappear when *we* appear.

Those who remember the Abu Ghraib scandals in 2003 and 2004 will be familiar with this story. Abu Ghraib prison, located in Iraq, has been a source of controversy for many years. The prison is best known for systemic abuse of prisoners at the hands of U.S. government military personnel and contractors. This abuse included physical cruelty, humiliation, psychological torture, rape, and sexual violence against detainees. The Abu Ghraib incident was seen as one of the most horrific violations of human rights, as it resulted in physical and psychological harm to prisoners who were denied basic rights such as access to representation or legal counsel during their imprisonment.

The scandal revealed how soldiers had breached ethical standards when dealing with prisoners and sparked international outrage over practices such as forced nudity, sleep deprivation, and beatings. During the investigation, 17 soldiers and officers were relieved of duty, and 11 were charged with battery, maltreatment, and aggravated assault. Other personnel were dishonorably discharged, imprisoned, reprimanded for dereliction of duty, or demoted. However, here are some facts that will help you understand the severity of the Abu Ghraib scandal. American soldiers committed the following acts:

- Urinating on prisoners.
- Jumping on an injured prisoner's leg with such force that it cannot heal.
- Pouring phosphoric acid on prisoners.
- Sodomizing prisoners with a baton.
- Attaching a rope to detainees' legs or genitals and dragging them.

Philip Zimbardo, a renowned social psychologist, served as an expert witness in the Abu Ghraib trials. Due to his involvement in the Stanford Prison Experiment, which in some ways reflected the abuse of power at Abu Ghraib Prison, Zimbardo was an ideal candidate. In 1971, Zimbardo conducted a psychological experiment to explore the impact of assuming the roles of both prisoner and guard, examining the effects of deindividuation and the influence of our assigned roles. In the Stanford Prison Experiment, college students participating in the study were assigned to take on the role of either a guard or prisoner in a simulated prison environment. The guards quickly began to behave aggressively, humiliating prisoners physically and mentally, just as at Abu Ghraib. The prisoners, on the other hand, were submissive and compliant, as is typical of individuals in those positions. Six days into the experiment, Zimbardo was forced to stop the study due to its horrendous and unethical conditions.

The Abu Ghraib scandal and the Stanford Prison Experiment demonstrate the power of deindividuation that people experience when they are in groups, as well as how people can become engulfed in their roles. Guards at Abu Ghraib inflicted cruel punishments on prisoners because they were less likely to feel guilty and remorseful when acting as a unit rather than individually. Deindividuation impacts many aspects of social interaction, including group dynamics and public morality. It can manifest itself in potentially dangerous situations, such as fraternity and sorority hazing, city riots, thieves ransacking stores and delivery trucks, and mob violence, in which some individuals no longer adhere to their own values. However, it is important to mention that we often align with certain groups because their values are similar to ours.

On January 6, 2021, an insurrection occurred at the Capitol Building when a group of people attacked and breached the building to disrupt Congress from certifying Joe Biden's election win. The events that transpired were shocking and have left many people questioning how such a thing could happen. One explanation is deindividuation, allowing members to feel anonymous and encouraging feelings of power and invulnerability that might otherwise be difficult to experience as an individual. Lost in the crowd, people exhibited risky and aggressive behaviors that would not usually occur if their identities were known. That being so, the attackers felt encouraged by their collective identity, which insulated them from feeling ashamed or liable for their behavior even though they had broken multiple laws to enter the Capitol Building. Sadly, seven people died due to the insurrection, and at least 114 law enforcement officers were injured. Perhaps the murder of Tyre Nichols by five Black police officers, who called themselves the Scorpion Unit, might now make more sense to you. As the officers took on their group identity and values as the Scorpion Unit, they temporarily lost their sense of self and moral culpability.

When a person's sense of self is lost or subsumed into a group, it diminishes their sense of personal responsibility. It can influence them to engage in more reckless behaviors than they would usually do on their own. Losing our identity can have negative consequences; it lowers our ability to think independently and make decisions based on our own moral code. As a result, we become more likely to conform to the actions of those around us without considering whether they are consistent with our values and beliefs.

Cognizant of the Circle

Although there is no one-size-fits-all answer regarding group dynamics, understanding their role in our lives and how they influence us is essential in developing our ideal selves and healthy relationships with those around us. Hopefully, by now, you understand how the need for belonging can be both beneficial and detrimental to us. Other people help us clarify our sense of self and build stable communities, but they may also encourage negative attitudes and behaviors.

Everyone strives to be part of a group. Groups profoundly impact how we interact with the world and help us form our identity. We are all born in the presence of others, and our social interactions and groups teach us who and what we are. In addition, relationships with close family and friends play a central role in developing our sense of self. As Roy Baumeister eloquently said, "A human being who spent his or her entire life in social isolation would almost certainly have a stunted and deficient self."[24]

As I mentioned earlier, we invariably create our own "looking-glass self," a view of ourselves that is influenced by how we believe others perceive us. Consequently, the views of others constantly influence what we think of ourselves and how we judge our self-worth and identity. When we adjust our actions to fit the *perceived* expectations or beliefs of others, we may develop an idealized image of ourselves or reinforce any prior negative feelings. However, the "looking-glass self" does have some positive aspects that I will discuss in Part Two of this book. We must consciously remember how the "looking-glass self" shapes our lives.

In addition to seeing ourselves through other people's eyes, we naturally curate environments that reinforce our attitudes and behaviors, further confirming our views of ourselves. However, we may unwittingly limit our growth and progress when we validate ourselves by only having friends with similar beliefs and tastes or only viewing media outlets with which we agree. Despite providing comfort and assurance that we are right, this narrow perspective is not conducive to personal growth. Why? Because these kinds of validating circles can close off the potential for open discussion and dialogue that can challenge our own ideas. Even if those different opinions do not necessarily sway us away from our original view, they can still offer valuable insights into how others think differently than us, a skill necessary in many creative thinking or problem-solving situations.

As with most other aspects of life, mimicking the behavior of others in order to gain acceptance or other rewards has advantages and disadvantages. Conformity can be beneficial and necessary in certain situations, like keeping the law, but it can also be dangerous, as the Abu Ghraib scandal demonstrates. In a similar vein, we can become lost in a larger collective and lose sight of our personal values, goals, and actions. Due to this increased anonymity or deindividuation—the feeling that we cannot be identified or singled out within a group—we may engage in behaviors we would not normally act out when alone.

Throughout this chapter, my goal was to help you become aware of your natural tendencies toward groups. At one time, all the factors discussed in this

> **Being cognizant of who and what influences us is a critical life skill.**

chapter entangled my old self and made it difficult for me to become who I am today. This is because our group experiences become a part of our autobiographical memory, and those memories inform our narrative identity. Therefore, being cognizant of who and what influences us is a critical life skill. It allows us to become aware of which people, groups, and activities positively or negatively affect our beliefs and behaviors. Whether we are conscious of it or not, we are all surrounded by a "circle of influence." This circle can include friends, family, co-workers, classmates, neighbors, teachers, members of your faith community, and even total strangers—anyone who may somehow affect our thoughts and actions. Taking the time to reflect on the people in this circle can help us determine which relationships are worth investing in and which may need to be reevaluated or discarded. By recognizing the sources of influence around us, we can become more intentional about what and who we accept into our lives.

This chapter completes Part One of this book. I hope you now have a framework for better understanding what people and events have influenced and shaped who you are. So, consider this a personal invitation to stay with me. In Part Two of this book, my goal is to help you take all the psychological information you've absorbed thus far and use it to start shaping and molding your future and who you will become. You will learn to use my nimble concept, just as I did, to design your life and move toward your *ideal self*—so you will flourish, feel more fulfilled, and have more meaningful relationships. See you in the following chapter!

Chapter Three Reflection Questions

1. Now that you've realized you see yourself through the eyes of others and seek social validation, describe some social characteristics that your peers or group members have. Explain whether their personal qualities are worthy and contribute to human flourishing.

2. Give an example of a time when you conformed to your peers to the point of blindly adopting the group's identity. How do you feel about your actions now that you have learned about conformity and deindividuation? *Note: consider carefully because people often believe they do not conform.*

REORGANIZING THE ASSOCIATED INFLUENCES; BECOMING THE ARCHITECT

4

Changing the Narrative

Re-Authoring Stories

In the 1980s, a groundbreaking therapeutic approach called *Narrative Therapy* emerged, spearheaded by Michael White and David Epston. They revolutionized the counseling and psychotherapy community by insisting that people must be separated from their problematic or destructive behaviors to receive adequate treatment. For example, when treating people who have committed crimes, White and Epston encourage them to think of themselves as individuals who have made mistakes rather than as inherently bad people. Their innovative approach challenged traditional notions that individuals are defined by their actions and instead emphasized the power of personal agency and resilience.

The goal of narrative therapy is to serve as a catalyst for re-writing the stories of our lives, acknowledging that our identities aren't static but ever-changing. It challenges the dominant narratives that are forced upon us or that we have imposed on ourselves. Narrative therapists recognize that each person has a unique story with multiple perspectives and interpretations.

I have a friend named Gabe, who spent many years in the military. Despite being an infantry officer, he often took on an unofficial chaplain role, providing counsel and support to his fellow military comrades who were struggling because of what they experienced. His commitment to the Christian faith motivated him to minister to the needs of others. After the terrorist attack on 9/11, Gabe was tasked with body recovery efforts at the Pentagon, an experience that left a lasting mark on him. Having spent so much time caring for others, Gabe had been unaware of his own internal struggles, which began to surface many years after leaving the military. Due to psychological and emotional issues caused by his experiences, he sought the assistance of a narrative therapist to help reframe his understanding of his story and integrate it into a broader narrative. Today, Gabe is a pastor, and he has more clarity about his experiences and recognizes how his journey has contributed to the larger story of his life.

Narrative therapy refrains from labeling individuals as "bad or broken." Instead, it encourages them to delve into their underlying motivations, fears, and desires—which helps people identify alternative narratives and develop healthier ways of relating to themselves and others. Instead of focusing on what is wrong with us, narrative therapy highlights our strengths, skills, and values. As a side note, this same philosophy underpins positive psychology, emphasizing our innate capacity for change and self-improvement. Nevertheless, by shifting our attention toward what we do well and what gives meaning to our lives, we gain agency over our personal narratives and become active authors of change.

In a nutshell, narrative therapy creates space for growth and transformation by recognizing that our actions are not always an accurate reflection of who we are. We all make mistakes, but those missteps do not have to define us; they can represent temporary detours on our journey toward becoming our ideal selves. When we understand that we can separate ourselves from our destructive patterns, we can take control of our lives and embrace a narrative filled with hope, resilience, and potential to create the life we truly desire.

> **We all make mistakes, but those missteps do not have to define us; they can represent temporary detours on our journey toward becoming our ideal selves.**

Despite my favorable opinions of narrative therapy, I disagree with some aspects, such as the postmodernist notion that there is no objective truth and that social norms and beliefs determine what is true. Although I may have these reservations, I appreciate the transformative potential of narrative therapy in empowering individuals to reclaim authorship over their own lives. It offers a refreshing perspective that acknowledges the influence of social norms while emphasizing personal agency in rewriting one's life story. Using narrative therapy as a framework, the following pages are aimed at helping you rewrite your story.

The turning point in my life occurred at the age of 19, sparking the beginning of rewriting my story. I had moved to Murfreesboro, Tennessee, to attend Middle Tennessee State University purely to escape my surroundings. I never expected to graduate from college because I thought I was intellectually inept, but I was open to the possibility that I might get a degree through sheer luck. In my freshman year, I shared a dorm with a student named Rich, who was about six years older than me, 25 at the time. We became good friends. Rich also had a friend named Leroy who lived across the hall; both were weed-smoking, music-loving, deep thinkers. Although I wasn't a big marijuana smoker, I'd sit around and listen to them talk, and their conversations and approach to life inspired me.

Rich and Leroy were brilliant, went to class, and were nothing like the guys I used to hang out with on the streets— trying to be tough or chase after every girl they saw. They knew how to embrace the present moment and enjoyed exploring black heritage festivals, African-American literature, black art, and jazz music. They always looked forward to attending open mic nights to see conscious hip-hop and spoken word performances. This was the first time I saw guys who looked like me living what seemed to be a better way of life; simple things fulfilled them, and their lives had meaning. My life soon started taking a new shape as I engaged in their conversations, observed their behaviors, and connected within their circles.

The first influencers who *unknowingly* helped me reauthor my story were Rich and Leroy. Although it is not always easy to let go of old attitudes and behaviors, we do tend to mimic those around us, particularly those with whom we spend the most time. I found myself aspiring to Rich and Leroy's level of depth and seeing my old habits as something to be buried. In retrospect, the lesson I learned from them is to see things as they *could be* rather than solely as they are.

Reauthoring serves as a metaphor for taking control of our life narratives, accepting our past experiences, and shaping a new path forward that would not materialize without our conscious efforts. Choosing what to write is one of the most challenging aspects. In many ways, it is like the book that you are currently reading. Sometimes, I sat down only to spend hours staring at a blank page, feeling like ideas, themes, and words had taken a hiatus. At those times, however, I simply wrote whatever came to mind and considered my overall intentions, which were to assist people in changing their narratives and becoming their ideal selves. Taking action led to motivation, and writing led to ideas. (I'll discuss action momentarily).

Similarly, when I moved to Murfreesboro for college, I had no clue how my life story would transpire or who I'd become; I simply desired to be a better person and realize my full potential and purpose (my overall intentions). With time, I became more determined to achieve my goals. As I developed relationships with the right people, ideas formed about who I could be. It all started with inspiration, then action, leading to motivation and ideas.

Maybe my situation speaks to you. You want to rewrite your story but are unsure how to begin or what to put on the pages. That's alright! I want you to think about your overall intentions, which are broad enough to get you close to where you want to be. Suppose, for example, "the West" represents your intentions; then you should head West. Don't worry too much about the details of your story; they'll emerge on their own. Instead, let your goals for becoming a better version of yourself serve as your guiding compass.

Your narrative is yours; therefore, you should be an expert in your own life. One of the primary goals of narrative therapy is to help us find our voices and use them for our own benefit. Expanding our perspectives and adopting healthier narratives can create more meaningful experiences, better understand ourselves, and become more socially productive. We can explore the stories we tell ourselves and challenge any negative beliefs that hold us back. Ultimately, narrative therapy reminds us that we have the power to shape our own narratives in a way that aligns with our values and aspirations.

Diagnosing Your Past, Designing Your Future

In part one, we spent a lot of time discussing the things that impacted our lives, and we learned that understanding how our past has shaped us is key to rewriting our stories. By identifying specific events

> **By identifying specific events that shaped us, for better or worse, we can intentionally organize the elements we need to create our desired future.**

that shaped us, for better or worse, we can intentionally organize the elements we need to create our desired future—seeing things as they could be.

The environment and social ties were the primary factors that influenced my early narrative. For instance, my father turned to crime, shattering our family and leaving us struggling to survive without him. Poverty was a constant companion. As a result, my mother was forced to care for three boys on her own while working as a secretary at a hospital for $9 an hour. She also cleaned homes in wealthy white communities and catered on the side to make ends meet. As a child, I watched her serve food, scrub toilets, and clean bathrooms. These challenges forced me to confront difficult realities at an early age.

Drugs and gangs provided additional layers to the complex storylines unfolding in my neighborhood and city. Peer pressure led many teens in our community down dangerous paths. As I pointed out earlier, my older brother succumbed to these dark forces, becoming involved with drug dealing and gangs and spending his adolescence and adulthood in and out of prison. My younger brother also sold drugs as a teen, was expelled from high school, and barred from attending any other high school in the county. Even close friends were victims of this bleak reality, turning from innocent playmates to convicted felons or, in the worst-case scenario, killed.

I also grew up when racism and police brutality were rampant and witnessed deep-seated prejudice firsthand. As a high schooler, I remember watching the Rodney King beating on TV in 1991 and thinking about my own problems with the police. All these factors impacted my life early and exposed me to the negative aspects of social pressure.

My past was shaped by *bottom-of-the-barrel conditions* occurring in broken environments lacking good leadership, opportunities, and resources. When people are subjected to these kinds of factors, they become frustrated and may behave in ways that are not beneficial to themselves or others, such as using unhelpful methods to solve problems, resorting to violence, or surviving by any means necessary. In addition to socioeconomic disparities, poor choices can contribute to such conditions. Negative influences are often associated with bottom-of-the-barrel conditions due to socioeconomic stress. Moreover, individuals in these circumstances tend to have an incomplete picture of human flourishing—it's difficult to thrive when all you want is to survive. Even Abraham Maslow recognized this reality, indicating that lower-level needs must be satisfied before people pursue higher-level ones. In other words, before considering self-actualization, we must first address our biological and safety needs.

On the bright side, bottom-of-the-barrel conditions *can* inspire activism to effect social change, such as the civil rights movement. And, as in my case, some individuals may see the desperation of their surroundings and aspire to greater things. Whatever the case, breaking free from the negative influences of these conditions is extremely difficult.

I use the term *mindset disparity* to describe a gap in thinking between *how things are* and *how they should be*, which involves having less-than-ideal mental structures and associations that negatively affect our values, judgments, and beliefs about the world. Although mindset disparities may be common in communities with limited opportunities, they can also exist in environments that teach racism, crime, excessive self-gratification, and self-hatred to children and teens, causing them to develop antisocial and maladaptive habits. Importantly, folks who live in poverty are not more likely to act immorally, just as those living in abundance are not more likely to act morally. Despite being poor and growing up in impoverished circumstances, I saw my mother and grandparents live moral, God-fearing lives. They always encouraged me to do the right thing and trust God.

I'm curious about how you would diagnose your past and the influences that surrounded you. Imagine how much deeper you would understand your narrative if you could identify the sources of your perceived problems. Earlier, I mentioned in Part One that the mind was designed to label things to simplify and organize our surroundings. Interestingly, I've never seen a doctor treat an illness without giving it some sort of diagnosis—that is, labeling it. Similarly, if you want to create the future you desire, you must diagnose and learn from your past. Winston Churchill once said, "Those who fail to learn from history are doomed to repeat it." I hope you will think about your past influences; the insights I gained from doing so have resulted in an untold number of positive changes for me.

Labeling these influences, on the other hand, does not have to be as elaborate as my example. It can be as simple as naming overarching themes that have impacted your life over time. My wife, for example, describes her childhood influence in terms of an environment that created an extreme need for approval from her parents, grandparents, and other authority figures. Her approval-seeking attitude caused her to feel self-conscious and lack confidence in her decisions, resulting in excessive people-pleasing behaviors.

We can identify significant events, experiences, and relationships that have affected our behavior by delving into our personal histories. These influences include childhood experiences, family dynamics, cultural background, upbringing, and even traumatic events. When we recognize these factors, we can better understand why we behave in certain ways and how these factors affect our relationships and personal stories. For instance, having been betrayed in the past can unconsciously leave a person with trust issues, affecting their ability to establish and maintain meaningful relationships. Acknowledging this connection can be a step toward healing, rebuilding trust, and designing a better future.

When we understand how past influences have shaped our narratives, we can learn to develop self-compassion. Through reflection, we may realize that some reactions are not entirely our fault but rather rooted in past circumstances beyond our control. We can also work toward personal growth by consciously addressing negative behavioral patterns and developing healthier ones, creating a new narrative for ourselves. The fact remains that although knowledge is great, it goes only so far. To change your life for the better, you must decide to act.

Gasping for Air

Permit me to digress for a moment. In my early twenties, I was fascinated by exotic saltwater fish and owned a small aquarium. One day, I found a fish dead on the floor; it had jumped out of the tank. Over the years, other fish died on me; some tried to leap out, but most of the time, I would find them floating, dead. Eventually, I gave up on the aquarium because I could never figure out what I was doing wrong.

I recently thought about that fish that jumped out of the tank twenty years ago. Finding the thought odd, I decided to investigate it. One of the main reasons fish leap out of their tanks is that the water doesn't have enough oxygen. Simply put, the tank water must have a high level of dissolved oxygen for the fish to breathe. Unfortunately, the natural balance between oxygen production and consumption can be disrupted in an aquarium. As a result, when fish sense this lack of oxygen, they instinctively try to leap out of the tank in search of an adequately oxygenated environment.

Despite being a late bloomer in aquarium science, I finally discovered why my fish jumped out of the tank over two decades ago: it was gasping for air! In a human voice, I imagine the fish thinking, "I'd rather die in search of a new environment than suffocate to death in this one." It is fascinating that even fish can detect when their environment will lead to their demise. In truth, I applaud the fish I discovered dead on my floor, leaping for a new home. In some ways, the leaping fish was compelled to survive by something deeper, resulting in a Hail Mary effort. As it is known in American football, a Hail Mary is an extremely long forward pass thrown in desperation—with a very low chance of being completed. Similarly, the leaping fish made a last-ditch effort.

This fish analogy rang true in my own life. Figuratively speaking, each time I changed my environment, I did so because I was gasping for air. We can all experience situations and environments that suffocate us physically, mentally, emotionally, relationally, and professionally. My move to Murfreesboro for college was a Hail Mary; it was either I die in my old environment or find an adequately oxygenated one. Likewise, after ten years in the Nashville area, I felt mentally, relationally, and professionally suffocated. In response, I jumped again in another desperate effort to move to Charlotte, North Carolina, with only three months' worth of living expenses and no real job prospects. Either gasp for air in Nashville or take another life-leaping risk.

Unfortunately, I hit rock bottom soon after moving to Charlotte, much like the fish on the floor, except I wasn't dead. I found part-time work as a personal trainer. However, a local gang known as MS-13 stole my car a few months after I moved, with my training equipment in the trunk. So, not only did they take my mobility, but they also took away my means of earning money. Although I've bounced back and then some, jumping to a new oxygen-filled environment isn't always without bumps and bruises, some of which can make you feel like you've lost your breath. Unlike the fish, though, we can get up and keep trying!

"Gasping for air" should motivate us to change our lives. When we feel suffocated by life's circumstances, we have two options: figuratively die in our current circumstances or take risks searching for new ones. Leaping to find oxygen does not necessarily imply a change in one's environment; it might simply mean adjusting our lifestyle in ways that meet our needs and goals better. Maybe you've made some poor decisions that are causing you to suffocate mentally and physically. Perhaps a relationship is sucking the wind out of you emotionally. Or you may feel professionally constrained and out of breath in your current job. It may be time to leap! If our current conditions are causing oxygen depletion, we may have nothing to lose and everything to gain.

Changing our narrative is critically dependent on constructive action. To change how we see ourselves and our place in the world, we must engage in behaviors that have the potential to produce positive outcomes. Constructive acts are the work behind the scenes that helps us to improve our lives. They are where the rubber meets the road. For example, a friend recently called to ask how he could improve his time management skills. He was convinced that his lack of proper time management hindered his ability to reach his full potential and robbed his family of the person he could become. After helping him identify the meaningful reasons for changing his behavior, I told him to write them on his bathroom mirror and look at them daily. I also instructed him to set aside two uninterrupted hours each week to focus on the important things to him. As a final step, I asked him to report back to me in two weeks to confirm he had completed the tasks—these are examples of constructive activities: establish your reasons, implement a plan, and ensure accountability. We can achieve long-term transformation only by rolling up our sleeves and getting to work.

> **To change how we see ourselves and our place in the world, we must engage in behaviors that have the potential to produce positive outcomes.**

Narrative Audits

Because we are *nimble*, we can recognize the power of choice and take responsibility for our decisions. In Part One, we learned that genetics, environment, and past experiences influence our choices in a variety of ways. As we question beliefs that hold us back, enhance our values, and pursue personal growth, we can begin to construct our reimagined narrative. To be an effective undertaking, however, we must first identify some existing narratives that have hindered us along the way. So, I came up with the idea of a narrative audit, as you might remember from Chapter 2.

Narrative audits involve examining personal content that sparks memories of recurring story themes in our lives and assessing these narratives' impact on us. Personal content can include memorable smells, specific locations, homes, particular movies and songs, photos, or anything else with sentimental value. These things can evoke memories of past experiences, which can be both positive and negative, and it's important to recognize how these events shaped our lives. A narrative audit can be performed more easily by analyzing photographs. Nevertheless, we can also consider any narrative theme that arises from other personal content.

A core component of narrative audits is *decentering*, a fundamental strategy for change within Mindfulness-Based Cognitive Therapy. When we decenter, we step away from our own mental events and view ourselves objectively, somewhat like a neutral, third-party observer would. In this way, we can examine the stories we tell ourselves and see how they affect our overall quality of life. For example, professional athletes step back and objectively review game films to observe what went down on the field instead of what they think played out.

Companies have often invited me to speak to their staff, and before finishing this chapter, I used my narrative audit idea to gather more insight and understanding. I was confident that I could help the participants develop a narrative-based self-awareness. Surprisingly, these were the most interesting parts of my presentation.

I would first demonstrate the audit by sharing details about narrative themes arising from my past photos, which made me feel a bit vulnerable. Then, I'd have my audience look through old photos of themselves on their phones and answer the following questions:

1. In reflecting on these photos, what overarching themes, past or present, come to mind regarding personal narratives that you told yourself or expressed to others? (Reconnect with the feelings and experiences surrounding the photo.)
2. What words would you use to describe the recently discovered narrative and its negative effect or benefit on your life at the time? (Be descriptive in your evaluation.)
3. Assume the person in the photos is not you. What words of wisdom would you impart to them in the hope they would change their attitude and behaviors to reshape future narratives? (Be specific.)

After my audience conducted their narrative audits, we discussed them on the spot. One of the most surprising elements of doing these live narrative audits was how emotional some people became. I then engaged with their deep emotional matters in real time. Some people would tear up as specific photos brought back emotions and revealed personal insecurities or other issues. The images became powerful tools to help each individual process their emotions. Some people admired how much they had grown and changed since the picture was taken and saw the photos as milestone markers that provided them with hope and revealed their resilience, while others were still trying to find their way and create new narratives.

One response on one of these occasions caught me off guard. After a narrative audit, a young Muslim woman wearing a hijab stated with tears in her eyes that she had searched her phone and could not find a single photo of herself. In a crowded room, she said she had not taken a photo in years because she wasn't sure she wanted to exist. Tears streamed down her face as she admitted to struggling with low self-esteem, attributing it to the influence of her social and cultural surroundings. It was so quiet in the room that you could hear a pin drop. My eyes teared up as well, and I struggled to speak. When I regained my composure, I looked her in the eyes and attempted to offer encouraging words before asking if we could talk after the event, as I was only halfway through my presentation.

Unfortunately, I can't provide closure on the young lady because I don't have it; she left immediately following my talk, and no one in the corporation knew who she was. I contacted HR, a manager, and team members in an attempt to locate her. I even emailed the CEO and executive staff about her and received no response. As her words and emotions had suggested, she was socially invisible.

Social invisibility occurs when individuals are disregarded, marginalized, or intentionally overlooked, negatively influencing their personal identity and place of belonging within society. A person who feels socially invisible has likely had their voice and experiences continually ignored. Without acceptance and social connection, we might think that our stories don't matter or aren't valued, which can make us feel alone and contribute to mental health problems like depression and anxiety. Consequently, we may develop feelings of powerlessness and stop viewing our narratives as ongoing. As the young woman in my audience experienced, *narrative foreclosure* occurs when we find our stories no longer relevant and no longer tell ourselves stories about ourselves (more on that in a moment).

Rewriting our stories becomes more difficult when we no longer see a good reason to live. In such cases, narrative therapy can offer hope. If the narrative audit becomes too emotionally challenging, it could necessitate the assistance of experts. My recommendation to those suffering from this level of mental trauma is to seek the assistance of a narrative therapist or a cognitive-behavioral therapist. Sometimes, another perspective and interpretation can help individuals make sense of their past experiences and chart a path toward a more meaningful future.

Following the narrative audit portion of my presentations, I ask participants to take selfies and schedule a reminder on their phones to perform another narrative audit in six months. I encourage them to engage in this practice twice a year, assessing and adjusting their perception of themselves in light of the narratives they have constructed. Our personal narratives shape our worldview and, ultimately, our quality of life.

> **Our personal narratives shape our worldview and, ultimately, our quality of life.**

Narrative auditing puts us in the driver's seat, where we can intentionally monitor the narratives we live by and become the architects of our own stories. This introspective practice allows us to identify the self-imposed limitations and counterproductive narratives that prevent us from reaching our full potential. We can challenge and reframe negative narratives into empowering ones through narrative audits.

When Self-Narratives End

Auditing helps maintain a certain quality and standard. A thorough audit can identify problems and discrepancies that might otherwise go unnoticed. It can also provide insights into potential areas for improvement and minimize future errors and inefficiencies.

I remember the first time the IRS audited me. I was in my mid-twenties and had learned to file my own taxes. When I learned I would be audited, I was terrified because I knew I had intentionally omitted a few 1099 forms to get more money back on my tax return. The audit revealed the missing 1099s, and after their adjustment, I ended up owing the IRS money. As you might expect, I learned my lesson and made things right. However, the audit identified the absence of 1099s, which were expected to be present.

In some ways, this auditing story resembles the young Muslim woman in my audience. After conducting her narrative audit, she discovered that she had no photos of herself to examine. The narrative audit, like the IRS audit, revealed the absence of a narrative that was expected to be included, and she was facing the consequences for lacking it; she was unsure about whether she wanted to live. *Narrative foreclosure* happens when someone believes that their life story can't be changed much by new interpretations of the past, new commitments in the present, or new experiences in the future.[25] Essentially, the person ceases creating new narratives about themselves and adopts the belief that they are incapable of making substantial changes to their life story.

Storytelling is an essential aspect of human experience. It transcends culture and time– everyone loves a good story. Narratives are told in various forms across all cultures; some are conveyed orally, others written down. Storytelling binds us together as human beings. Through stories, we find meaning in our experiences and relate to one another's struggles and triumphs. So, when we repeat negative narratives about ourselves and neglect to embrace new, positive narratives, we find ourselves on a lonely, empty road that may lead to death.

When my mother's health deteriorated significantly, I witnessed narrative foreclosure firsthand. Like the young woman in my audience, she stopped telling herself new stories about herself. Following a series of medical procedures, she found herself immobile and confined to her apartment's small bedroom, unable to cook or properly care for herself. One evening, when I arrived in town, I discovered she was starving after not eating since the day before. She was deprived of the attention she needed from other family members, and you can imagine how heartbroken I was. After years of pleading with her to relocate temporarily to Charlotte so I could assist her, she finally agreed.

When she arrived, she struggled to climb my steps, gasping for breath. I immediately changed her regimen, including her eating habits. I'd wake her up in the mornings and open the window to let in as much light as possible because she was used to lying in her dark room all day. I also assembled the best medical team for her. I even went so far as to purchase a massage table to help stretch her legs and back, and I encouraged her to walk several times a week. She also started attending church with us, enjoyed being outdoors while I grilled, and loved grabbing a beer and listening to music with me.

One important factor involved changing her medication, which had caused her legs to give out. And after she graduated from physical therapy, I signed her up for a gym membership, and she'd go with me twice a week. She usually finished before me and enjoyed observing others working out in the gym while patiently waiting for me. I'll never forget her beaming smile when I walked around the corner when it was time to leave.

As you probably can sense, my mother began telling herself a new story—that she could have a healthy social life and contribute to those around her. She started watching our boys when my wife and I went out on date nights or whenever we needed it. She also began to help with dishes and other minor household tasks and even cooked a few meals. After nine months, my mother felt confident and ready to return home with a new outlook, improved health, and social vitality. Her foreclosure story evolved into a *redemption narrative,* in which the main character experiences pain or setbacks but ultimately becomes better or stronger in some way.[15]

Everyone loves redemption stories. A story that takes our sorrows and turns them into triumphs and our failures into successes. Redemption stories give us hope and teach us to learn from our setbacks and come out of them stronger. It's a story of resilience and courage in the face of adversity, and it's a story that reminds us that we can conquer even the most difficult circumstances.

Everything considered, it is worthwhile to acknowledge my mother's genetic predispositions, such as disc degeneration causing lumbar spinal stenosis and environmental conditions that exacerbated depression and anxiety. She had to become *nimble* and change her environment, habits, and mindset in order to transform her situation.

So, will you give in to unhelpful narratives that rob you of the person you want to be? Will you resign to narrative fore-closure, believing your story is irrelevant? Or will you create a story of redemption? Like my mother, you have a choice to make. And with work, you can change your narrative, just as she did. Now, let's construct who you aspire to be! I'll see you in the next chapter!

Chapter Four Reflection Questions
The Narrative Audit
(Instructions)

Find pictures of yourself with emotional value that evoke memories of a particular season in your life. It doesn't matter if the photos were taken a week or five years ago as long as you can find a narrative theme. Next, evaluate the images as objectively as possible using the following questions: (You may also seek assistance from close friends, family members, mentors, counselors, and therapists.)

1. In reflecting on these photos, what overarching theme comes to mind regarding personal narratives you told yourself or expressed to others? (Reconnect with the feelings and experiences surrounding the photo.) These themes can be past or present.

2. What words would you use to describe the recently discovered narrative and its negative or beneficial effect on your life at the time the photos were taken? (Be descriptive in your evaluation.)

3. Assume the person in the photos is not you. What words of wisdom would you impart to them, hoping they could change their attitudes and behaviors to help shape future narratives? (Be specific.)

4. Embrace this newfound attitude or behavior and implement it in your daily life.

5. Additionally, seek out a trustworthy partner with a growth mindset and a strong passion for lifelong learning to help hold you accountable when going through a narrative audit.

Yours To Design: Constructing a Life That is Meaningful

(For re-evaluation)

Take a selfie right now and conduct a narrative audit again in six months (set a reminder on your phone). Then, repeat this process every six months. Look for a theme.

5

Constructing Yourself

Clearing the Fog

I have always been fascinated by fog and its pervasiveness, especially when it is thick. Yet, I am aware of its destructive potential. It's a mysterious phenomenon that can obscure visibility and distort reality. Fog contributes to roughly 25,000 automobile crashes each year. My heart sinks when I hear about a multi-car pileup triggered by fog. It reminds me of my own vulnerability because I've also been in similar road conditions but escaped unharmed.

The main factor responsible for these accidents is that people have a decreased reaction time to sudden changes in traffic patterns or unexpected obstacles. Reduced visibility can set off a chain reaction, resulting in devastating pileups, causing severe injuries, or even loss of life. Recent news reported that a dense "super fog" had blanketed New Orleans, causing a major pileup involving 168 vehicles. The incident resulted in over 63 injuries, some of which were severe, and claimed the lives of eight individuals. Additionally, there were reports of vehicle fires and a hazardous material-carrying truck being involved. Authorities confirmed that the "super fog" was a major factor in the accidents.

Although fog may present many challenges, it also carries a profound metaphorical meaning. Foggy perspectives can distort our perceptions of ourselves and disrupt our reactions to particular situations. Many people are lost in a fog of confusion and uncertainty about their lives. At some point, we've all questioned our purpose, identity, and place in the world; perhaps you are doing so right now. These challenges can undermine our motivation and leave us unsure of how to navigate the complexity of life. A lack of clarity about our place in the world can cloud our aspirations, making it difficult to achieve our dreams. Also, navigating our social interactions effectively becomes challenging when we lack self-understanding. Therefore, we must be clear about what we *want* in life to avoid complacency, indecisiveness, maladaptive behaviors, and interpersonal difficulties.

Knowing what we value in life is critical, so our decisions reflect our values. Without this awareness, we risk conforming to societal expectations and the opinions of others, leading to a superficial existence rather than being who we desire to be. By trying to please others, we can lose sight of who we are and what matters most to us, limiting our growth and potential. When our outlook is hazy, it's harder to acknowledge our biases, creating further negative consequences in our personal and professional lives.

Just like physical fog impairs one's ability to react quickly and decisively while driving, *psychological* fog similarly affects our responses when facing challenges, overcoming hardships, or seizing opportunities. Furthermore, being unclear about our identity can result in diminished self-worth, tense interpersonal connections, uncertainty about our professional paths, and overall discontentment with life. These consequences can "pile up" over time, causing great emotional pain, mental health issues, damage to our relationships, and other detrimental effects in our lives. Because we have a basic need for a stable environment and a secure sense of self, we are inevitably thrown into disarray when we feel unsure about ourselves and the world around us.

Clearing the fog begins with acknowledging its presence and potential danger and then realizing that we have the power to clear our internal haze. The road to clarity may entail confronting difficult questions about our beliefs, values, and behaviors, as well as developing a life vision for ourselves that integrates our personal, professional, and social lives in a meaningful way. Working through fears and traumatic experiences and reevaluating self-imposed limitations may be a part of the process of seeking clarity. To disrupt negative patterns and transform our outlook, we must critically reflect on our self-narratives, reorder our priorities, and undertake productive tasks that will enable us to meet our desired goals. For some, clearing the fog may involve therapy; for others, it may require self-reflection, introspection, and personal, environmental, and relationship changes. In both cases, a commitment to personal growth is essential.

Clearing the fog is not a one-off occurrence but rather an ongoing process that demands continual self-awareness and a willingness to learn from both triumphs and setbacks as we move forward. One more thing to remember: after the sun rises, the ground and air warm up, causing the air to be warmer than the dew point temperature, and the fog evaporates. So, sunlight clears the fog. To enrich our lives, we must continually seek light in order to gain a clearer perspective.

Choosing to be Rare

You will not be surprised to learn that reducing ambiguity in our lives requires conscious effort. Nevertheless, another dense cloud that prevents people from reaching their potential is that they spend too much time living on autopilot; they move through life without giving serious, conscious thought to who they are and who they are becoming. In a way, they jump from the driver's seat and allow life to just happen to them, accepting whatever life brings. Without self-direction, people tend to head in any direction, which can lead to a life of mediocrity in which people settle only for what life gives them instead of creating the life they want.

Many people, at least in Western society, are apathetic toward becoming their best selves and are more focused on instant gratification than on their personal growth. Their disinterest in growth stems from their preoccupation with technology, social media, attention-seeking lifestyles, the newest trends and fashion, and the next thrilling experience. Modern society bombards us with overwhelming stimulation that diverts our attention from the truly important things. Even at the corporate level, I have witnessed similar apathy where companies readily allocate significant funds toward *underutilized* resources and extravagant corporate functions but don't invest equally in their employees' personal growth.

One of my most persistent questions throughout all my studies has been why some people strive to reach their potential while others do not. I've often wondered how something so important as becoming the best version of yourself could be overlooked and ignored. Ironically, *everyone* wants "the best" of everything else, but many people fall short of this standard when it comes to themselves. We desire the *best* house, the *best* cars, the *best* clothes, and the *best* jobs, but fail in our efforts to become our *best* selves.

Abraham Maslow, who was deeply interested in personal growth questions, believed that mere "ordinary" people never stretch themselves to reach their full potential. Perhaps the distinction between ordinary people and those who are not explains why many fail to use their greatest abilities. Maslow argued that those who strive to reach their full potential are *actually* the ones who have transcended the so-called average or normal way of life.

Interestingly, people in *individualistic* societies value standing out over blending in. We strive to express our distinct personalities and highlight our unique abilities or characteristics to set ourselves apart from the crowd. Self-promotion is a common strategy for gaining recognition and admiration from other people. In modern Western society, we embrace our individuality through unconventional fashion choices or openly showcasing our personal qualities. However, despite all efforts to be different, those who fail to capitalize on their abilities are considered normal by Maslow's standards. He believed that self-actualized people were relatively rare in the general population.[26]

As described by Maslow, self-actualization represents a person's realization of their full potential, the pursuit of personal growth, and a strong interest in humanity and interpersonal relationships. It also involves qualities such as creativity, autonomy, a strong sense of ethics and values, problem-solving abilities, frequent peak experiences, and a deep sense of purpose.[27] He viewed self-actualization as a high level of psychological development and personal fulfillment that only a small percentage of people achieve. Although everyone can realize their full potential, Maslow believed that most individuals either don't pursue it or make only minimal progress due to their preoccupation with satisfying their basic needs and societal expectations.[26] I would also point out that some folks entertain too many distractions and frivolous pursuits, making it more difficult to reach their potential.

In my view, the pursuit of self-actualization begins with a choice. For example, I remember advising my younger sibling on how to deal with a moral situation. Though he agreed it was the right decision, he decided against it, remarking that I was rare and that most men would not do as I recommended. I told him, "I choose to be rare!" Ironically, many people believe those who achieve great things are born with extraordinary abilities, motivation, and discipline. In some cases, this is true, but most high achievers will tell you that they have worked hard to develop the characteristics that have contributed to their success and shaped who they are.

To reach our potential, we must *choose* to be the rare exception, even if it means making morally right decisions when others won't. Fully utilizing our *nimble* abilities involves recognizing the power of choice, grasping the immense possibilities of our talents and abilities, and sincerely pledging to utilize them for the betterment of ourselves and those around us. Self-actualized people take the road less traveled, make the right moral choices, and push themselves beyond their comfort zones and perceived limitations.

> **To reach our potential, we must choose to be the rare exception, even if it means making morally right decisions when others won't.**

The late psychiatrist William Glasser emphasized the importance of choice in his development of *Reality Therapy*, which helps individuals recognize their active role in contributing to their own problems. Glasser has written extensively about people's ability to participate actively in their own destinies. In his view, people adopt ineffective behaviors in an effort to satisfy specific desires and needs. However, we all have some control over what we continue to do. As a result, Glasser believed that although we may not *always* possess control over our emotions and thoughts, we do have control over our actions. By altering our actions, we enhance the likelihood of changing our emotions and thoughts.[28] We should be aware, though, that unconscious processes can influence our behavior without us even realizing it, making some actions more difficult to change.

Reality Therapy is built upon the principles of *Choice Theory*, which suggests that our actions are driven by our desire to fulfill basic needs such as *survival, love and belonging, power or achievement, freedom* or *choice*, and *fun*. Even seemingly self-destructive or irrational behaviors are viewed as efforts to satisfy these needs. Recognizing that all behavior is purposeful is a crucial element of Choice Theory because it fosters personal accountability and helps people make better decisions. When we acknowledge that underlying desires and needs drive behavior, we can focus on finding more constructive and fulfilling ways to satisfy them. Given these considerations, Choice Theory offers insights into how we can make effective choices to fulfill our needs.[29]

By recognizing that our *behavior, thinking, emotions,* and *bodily sensations* are all interconnected, we can effectively meet our needs through the concept of *total behavior*. According to Choice Theory, any change in one component can impact the others. For instance, a shift in our thinking can result in changes in our emotions as well as influence our physical reactions and behavior. As a result, Choice Theory aims to help people understand and take charge of their total behavior to make better decisions and improve their quality of life.[29]

To get what we want, we must become proactive, beginning with small changes in our thinking and actions. Our behavior and thinking are the only things we can directly control. So, to change how we feel emotionally and physically, we must make a deliberate effort to change what we do and think. Overall, Choice Theory stresses the importance of self-control to help people make responsible choices and take ownership of their own lives rather than dictating the decisions and lives of others.

Becoming the Architect

Throughout my personal journey from discontentment to fulfillment, I have consistently recognized the profound ramifications of Choice Theory. As a teenager, long before I understood Choice Theory, I realized the power of my choice-making ability. Although many of my peers sold drugs in the 90s, I *chose* to sell pagers and cell phones during their rise. By aligning myself with these emerging technologies, I achieved a lifestyle like my peers without breaking any laws. As a result, many of them admired me.

Meeting Darrell, the owner of Global Paging, where I worked, was a transformative experience that greatly shifted my perspective. Darrell hired me to sell pagers on the streets to prove myself before allowing me to work in the office. He held competitions among all his salespeople, and I won every month. Eventually, Darrell saw my success as an outside salesperson and promoted me to oversee his entire office. I was 17 years old. For two years, I observed his interactions with individuals from both the urban community and corporate settings. His ability to navigate these two distinct worlds effortlessly amazed me—and I aspired to possess the same qualities.

Darrell was my first mentor, and he played a significant role in who I've become. I am most likely an entrepreneur today because of him. Initially, I was oblivious to how much he influenced my life, as we all are sometimes. In most cases, we can see the profound impact that others have had on our lives only in retrospect. Since meeting Darrell, I've purposefully sought out other mentors to assist me in constructing who I want to be (more on that later). And over the years, I have continued to make *choices* to craft the life I want.

Have you ever stopped to think about the ripple effect caused by one decision? It's fascinating how a single choice can trigger a cascade of other decisions, shaping our lives positively or negatively. Frequently, I contemplate how my choices are linked together, with one decision serving as a foundation for subsequent ones. I also consider how my choices have shaped my life's path and have intertwined with and become a part of the narratives of other people's lives. As I did with Darrell, I'm curious if you can identify some good and bad decisions that have shaped who you are and where you find yourself today.

You have the ability to make choices that will empower you to become the architect of your life. Don't underestimate the true extent of your power. Alfred Adler, the late renowned Austrian psychologist, emphasized the *creative power* within each individual. In Adler's view, every person has an innate ability to shape and create their own way of life. He regarded human beings as active agents in their own lives, capable of making choices and controlling their circumstances. In essence, creative power is what constitutes a free individual.[27]

The *nimble* concept I developed is based on the notion of creative power. In Chapter 1, we explored how both inherited traits and environmental factors shape our characteristics. Nevertheless, Adler believed, as I do, that people are more than just a product of their genes and their environment. As creative beings, we have the power to respond to our environment, actively shape it, and influence it in ways that are beneficial to us; similar to how painters manipulate their canvases to achieve their desired results. As some personality theorists suggest, heredity and environment are the bricks and mortar of our personality, but architectural design is due to our own creative power. Essentially, the way in which we utilize our bricks and mortar has shaped who we are today.[27] In this respect, we are responsible for who we are, whom we become, and how we behave.

According to Adler, people have the ability to overcome obstacles and create a meaningful existence through their thoughts, actions, and attitudes. He emphasized that creativity encompasses all aspects of life, not just artistic expression. Our imaginative capacities can be harnessed and applied to many aspects of our lives. Furthermore, Adler proposed that people could use their creative abilities to turn challenges into opportunities for growth and change.

Adler's perspective aligns with a statement made by William James, the renowned philosopher and psychologist of the late 19th century, who is widely recognized as the pioneer of American psychology. His words can be paraphrased as follows: The hell that theology talks about is not worse than the hell we make for ourselves in this world by *shaping* our personalities in the wrong way. If young people knew how quickly they would turn into walking habits, they would be more careful about their actions while they are still malleable. We are choosing our fates, which can't be undone, for good or bad—in every small act of virtue or vice, there is a mark left behind.[30]

So, how are you shaping your personality? Are you cultivating qualities that lead to flourishing, or are you caught in a cycle of destructive behaviors? I agree with William James: our destinies are shaped by the choices we make, and the consequences of our decisions can leave indelible marks.

People often think that they must embark on a journey *to find* themselves when they lack clarity or have difficulties caused by their own choices that lead to unhappiness. Years ago, I began to question the merits of this idea. I almost jumped out of my chair when I heard a lecture by Elliot Aronson, a renowned social psychologist, who stated that *the self* is not something we find but something we construct. We construct ourselves through our behavior, making difficult decisions, and by what we do morally. According to Aronson, "Who am I?" is a good question, but a much better question is, "Who do I want to become?"[31]

The self is not something that can be found. However, we can learn about ourselves and go through a process of self-discovery. As we uncover these learned aspects of ourselves, we can choose to embrace them, work to discard them, or simply leave their imprint up to chance. Regardless, it is undeniable that we play a role in constructing ourselves, whether we are aware of it or not.

Looking back on my life over the last fifteen years, I made some specific attitude changes that helped construct who I am today. Using the acrostic *I.D.E.A.L.*, I have simplified my attitude approach into five core principles to help others live a life by design.

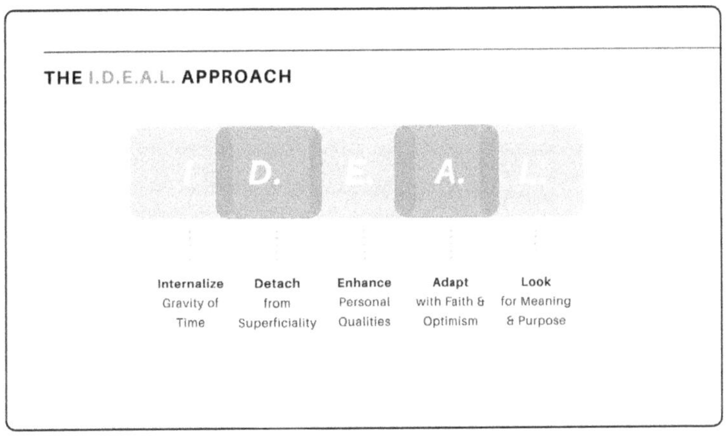

Figure 5.1 - The I.D.E.A.L. Approach to Becoming Your Ideal Self

The first thing I did was *Internalize the Gravity of Time*. I realized I was wasting far too much time doing and thinking about things that were handicaps to achieving my goals and becoming the person I desired to be. The significance of time struck me during a discussion with my father-in-law, who compared each day to 24 valuable bricks of gold that are available to everyone. Some people wisely use their bricks of gold to achieve meaningful and substantial outcomes, while others flush them away on unimportant and time-wasting activities.

The deceptive aspect of time is its small increments, which we are willing to squander. We tend to ignore the small moments that pass but become alarmed when they add up to a large sum. The large sum is cleverly concealed within the increments. Once again, the increments have the potential to be misleading.

Imagine mindlessly hitting the snooze button on your alarm clock every morning, believing that an extra 15 minutes of sleep won't matter. However, over the course of a month, those small increments of time add up to *hours* of lost productivity and chaotic mornings that leave you feeling stressed, which in turn impacts your mental health and relationships. Like most people, you wouldn't purposefully try to create these consequences; nevertheless, most of us overlook the importance of 15 minutes.

Various aspects of our lives illustrate the reality of ignoring time increments, including excessive use of social media, frequenting clubs or bars, associating with the wrong people, and habitually procrastinating on essential tasks needed to move us forward. As a result of our willingness to ignore *seemingly* insignificant things, we can squander *years'* worth of small increments of time.

Fifteen years ago, I found myself immersed in this very reality. I became proactive when I finally understood that every small moment contributed to the bigger picture. I committed to focusing on smaller increments of time, avoiding putting things off, steering clear of people and situations that waste time, and taking daily actions toward my goals. When I adopted this perspective, I made decisions more quickly that propelled me forward and developed a strong determination to persevere even when faced with difficult situations.

> **Time is a curse for a person in prison but a gift for someone with a purpose.**

We must recognize that time is our *most valuable* nonrenewable resource and consciously prioritize and utilize it wisely. It is intriguing how time is a curse for a person in prison but a gift for someone with a purpose.

The second thing I did was **Detach from Superficial Attachments**, which included distancing myself from certain people and places, avoiding surface-level conversations and interactions, and no longer being consumed by material possessions. Superficial attachments can mold our personalities, causing us to prioritize things of lesser worth while neglecting those that hold true value. We may even attach our self-worth to material things, creating a false sense of security and feelings of inadequacy when we don't possess them. We may also develop an object-oriented mindset and view people as mere tools, even exploiting them to satisfy our desires.

The late Jewish theologian and philosopher, Martin Buber's *Model of Relatedness*, comes to mind when considering the impact of superficial attachments. His model provides insight into how individuals can engage with others and establish meaningful connections. Buber identified two fundamentally different kinds of relationships that we may have with other people. The first is an *I-It relationship*, in which we view others as objects or a means to an end. In this mode, people see each other as separate entities with little regard for their intrinsic value as human beings. On the other hand, the I-Thou relationship represents a genuine encounter between individuals in which they fully recognize the uniqueness and dignity of others and appreciate each other's existence. In I-Thou relationships, individuals are not treated as objects or a means to an end but rather as ends in themselves. These relationships typically involve openness, empathy, and a deep sense of connection. Buber believed that the *I-It relationship* was the dominant mode of relationships in modern society.[32] From my perspective, the attitudes and behaviors that spawn I-It relationships arise due to a life enveloped in superficiality.

To transform my life, I realized I couldn't construct who I wanted to be on shaky ground. As a result, I developed an unwavering distaste for indulging in frivolous activities. Consequently, you'll never spot me partaking in the frenzy of Black Friday shopping or waiting eagerly in line for the latest footwear release. Nor will you find me socializing with individuals who have a negative impact on my life. My aspirations are clear: to embody purpose and foster genuine relationships.

Next, I put forth a lot of effort to *Enhance* my personal qualities. I realized that if I wanted to do more *with* my life, I needed to do more work *in* my life. It became clear that my place in the world directly resulted from my choices and the abilities I had honed. Inspired by Albert Einstein's explanation of insanity, which is doing the same things repeatedly but expecting different results, I decided to make a change. I started reading a lot, listening to lectures, taking online courses, pursuing certifications, connecting with exceptional individuals, finding mentors, and even re-enrolling in college. In addition, I worked hard to improve my intellectual abilities, skills, personality traits, and character strengths. As psychologist Carol Dweck highlights in her theory of the growth mindset, our personal attributes are not set in stone but can be changed through deliberate hard work.[33]

Many years ago, I read *The 21 Irrefutable Laws of Leadership* by John Maxwell, in which he discusses the *Law of the Lid*. Maxwell stated that our leadership ability determines our level of effectiveness. In other words, our potential for success is limited by our ability to lead others. He argued that the lid on our leadership capacity is a barrier, preventing us from reaching our full potential and achieving great results. Leaders with low lids struggle to make significant progress because they lack the necessary skills and mindset to lead effectively. On the other hand, leaders with high lids have developed strong leadership abilities and can effectively inspire and guide others toward success. Maxwell posited that the essence of leadership is influence; thus, lacking influence renders one incapable of leading.[34] Keep in mind that everyone is leading someone, whether it's members of their family, a community organization, a bible study group, or children's sports. Everyone has someone following them. As a result, our ability to lead those we care about is directly proportional to our level of self-leadership.

Looking back, I was at a place in life that corresponded to my lid or the cap of my abilities. How would you perceive your current standing in life relative to your lid? *The Law of the Lid* was eye-opening and a reminder that I needed to improve my abilities and raise my lid to maximize my impact and achieve greatness.

As I moved toward the person I wanted to be, I also had to *Adapt with Faith and Optimism*. The change wasn't easy. I frequently share with others that I had to learn how to walk, talk, and dress all over again because of the influence of my early surroundings. I also had to face individuals who knew my past and were familiar with the old me. Their ridicule made it seem like I was trying to be someone I was not or changing for the worse. As we move toward becoming the person we want to become, we have to unlearn some things; I had to learn to fight differently using my mind and social skills rather than physical aggression. I've also encountered a multitude of life hurdles, such as my daughter being diagnosed with a brain tumor at age five, my first marriage ending in divorce, civil legal issues, and my current wife's diagnosis of multiple sclerosis. I am grateful to share that my daughter had a successful brain surgery during that time. As I am penning this book, she is a wonderful young woman pursuing a college degree in post-natal nursing.

Over the years, I have also taken numerous entrepreneurial risks and embarked on failed ventures, resulting in significant financial hardships for my family. At times, I had no idea where my next paycheck would come from. It may surprise you to learn that in business, I have been told "no" way more than "yes." Amidst all these trials, I worked hard to maintain my self-confidence and unwavering faith in God, all the while holding onto hope that everything would eventually fall into place.

Shifting gears, a few years ago, I attempted to offer employee coaching services to a company headed by a CEO from the technology industry. He firmly believed in setting *measurable* goals to evaluate people's accomplishments, as shared by their HR executive. Consequently, he frequently stressed to his employees that *hope* cannot be measured, but I insisted to the HR director that it could.

The late Curt Richter, a biologist renowned for his experimental animal studies, made noteworthy contributions to the field of psychology. In his drowning rat experiments at Harvard in the 1950s, rats were placed in half-filled water tanks and given the opportunity to swim. However, after some time, they were exposed to conditions that made it extremely challenging or even impossible for them to escape. When faced with the inescapable conditions, the rats displayed learned helplessness, completely abandoned any attempt to swim, and showed a profound sense of resignation toward their predicament. In contrast, the rats rescued just before they were expected to die were placed back in the water, and this time, they could swim for 60 hours! Why? Richter concluded that when hope remained, the rats did not die.[35]

Other animal studies have demonstrated similar results. Perceiving a lack of control over one's environment or life circumstances can lead to feelings of hopelessness. When people or animals lose hope in their situation, they give up and stop trying to change or influence the outcome. It is critical that we all adapt with faith and optimism in order to keep moving forward.

Lastly, I took steps to **Look for Meaning and Purpose**. At the start of this book, I emphasized that unfulfillment caused me great emotional agony. During those years, I embarked on a desperate journey to uncover meaning and purpose because my very life depended on it. A lack of fulfillment is like a disease that spreads throughout the human soul, leaving us feeble,

> **A lack of fulfillment is like a disease that spreads throughout the human soul, leaving us feeble, dysfunctional, and empty.**

dysfunctional, and empty. And I felt the consequences of this meaninglessness in my relationships, job, and life. I'm sure you can recall similar experiences in your own life due to a lack of fulfillment.

I would even argue that, in many cases, those responsible for school shootings and other mass killings have a void when it comes to fulfillment in their lives. Our sense of self-worth stems from having a life of meaning and purpose, which is at the heart of our human existence. In fact, the French-Algerian philosopher Albert Camus believed that humans ceaselessly strive to convince themselves that their existence is not meaningless.[36]

Victor Frankl was a Holocaust survivor, psychiatrist, and neurologist who endured World War II concentration camps. His experiences in the concentration camps had a significant impact on his psychotherapeutic method known as logotherapy (or meaning therapy). He contended that humanity's primary motivation is to *search for meaning* rather than pleasure or power. In the concentration camps, he saw that it was not always the weakest or sickest who died but those who had lost faith and saw their lives as meaningless. Frankl became fixated on Friedrich Nietzsche's statement, "He who has a why to live for can bear with almost any how." He held the conviction that Nietzsche's assertion ought to serve as the guiding principle for all psychotherapy. For Frankl, a life of meaning is one that is strong enough to withstand even the Nazi death camps.[37]

We not only seek meaning but also create it. We can actively seek out and construct meaning and purpose in our lives by developing *compelling reasons* (or our why) to underpin the motivation for why we do anything. For instance, *my why* is to give God a return on investment for my life—this is the compelling reason that motivates and guides my work, relationships, and decisions. Bear in mind that meaning pertains to *understanding, value,* or *significance,* whereas purpose entails *directing toward an intentional end.* (I will delve deeper into purpose in the final chapter).

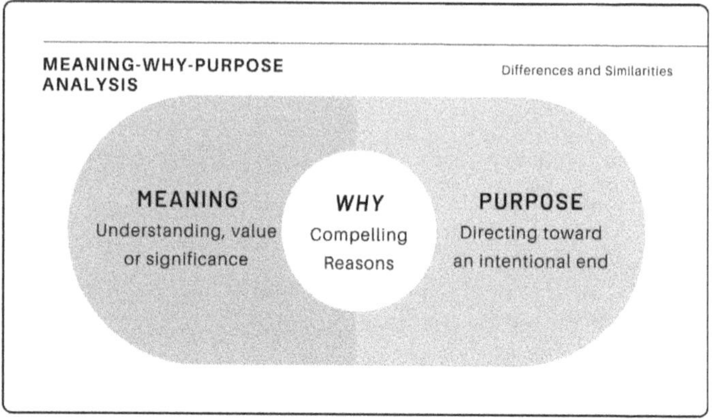

Figure 5.2 - Meaning-Why-Purpose Analysis

What activities are truly worth your time and valuable in your daily life? How can you enhance your personal attributes? What beliefs will inspire unwavering faith and optimism? Find the things that matter so you can grow meaning in your life and start to develop your compelling reasons. Keep in mind that your compelling reasons serve as a link between meaning and purpose. Just as I have done, you can use your compelling reasons as motivation to deliberately direct the meaningful things in your life in a way that designs the life you want to live. By transforming my attitude always to be mindful of meaning and purpose, I was able to cultivate more fulfillment in my life. By applying my *I.D.E.A.L.* framework, I have moved closer and closer to my *ideal self.* You can also use my approach to shape who you aspire to become.

Being the architect of your life means that you *direct it toward an intentional end.* Architects are purposeful; they are designers with a vision and know where they want to end up. Imagine a world with no architects; the built environment as we know it would be very different. Cities' skylines would not have the complex web of skyscrapers, modern technological marvels, and historic landmarks that have been a part of our urban landscapes for generations. Structures would no longer show the signs of well-thought-out design by fitting in with their surroundings and making the most of their usefulness. Instead, buildings would be a bunch of random pieces of raw materials, lacking the beauty and strength provided by architectural design. A world without architects would be devoid of the essence of human creativity and innovation in our surroundings, leaving us with a barren, monotonous environment. Perhaps it's because of this barrenness that the Bible says that without a vision, the people perish. So, what will become of your human landscape? Will it resemble a thoughtful, intentional design or a barren landscape?

Growing Your Empowerment Circle

As the architects of our lives, we must each make deliberate choices about the people we let in. We all intuitively sense that certain people are not good for us to be around, while others are. Like antivirus software on our computers, we should flag suspicious activities that could harm us and quarantine them. It's fascinating how our fight-flight-or-freeze response effectively warns us of physical danger. Still, we must also recognize the subtler threats posed by certain attitudes, thought patterns, and behaviors. As the New Testament scripture suggests, "bad company corrupts good character."[38]

Social influence is the area of social psychology that studies how people and groups affect our thoughts and actions. In the third chapter, I emphasized how the powerful pressure to conform can change our thoughts and actions. Furthermore, the specific *reference groups* with which we identify offer a continuous cycle of influence, shaping our attitudes and behaviors as we look to the group for information and norms to guide us. Typically, our reference groups include friends, family members, classmates, colleagues, and other important groups, such as college communities or religious groups who share our interests. We hold the opinions of people in our reference groups in particularly high regard, seek their approval, and look to them for direction. At the core, our reference groups guide our beliefs, values, and actions and shape our identity.

As a teenager, my reference group consisted of other street kids like me—kids that I desperately wanted to impress and be accepted by. Then, early in college, my reference group expanded to include people like Rich and Leroy, who challenged me to think more deeply. As I progressed through my college years, I gravitated toward a circle of philosophers and theologians whom I aspired to emulate. As you might expect, this pattern has persisted, but I am now purposefully choosing my social circle to align with the direction I want to take in life. (But more on that topic in a minute.) Have you considered how your connections with different reference groups shaped your identity, led you to see the world in particular ways, and influenced your behavior?

During my late twenties, more than a decade after I had Darrell as an important mentor, I began to think a lot about mentorship. As a result, I pursued significant one-on-one time with many of my professors to absorb as much knowledge and guidance as possible. Suddenly, I had a revelation: I realized that my mentors were like blueprints that I could copy, adapt, and make my own. After seeing how this process works, I discovered that I could also carefully select my reference groups, made up of mentors and inspiring individuals who could become my circle of empowerment. Consider the concept of the looking-glass self we covered in Chapter 3, indicating how we adopt views of ourselves that reflect how we think others perceive us. Perhaps the concept can apply to how we think our mentors and other inspiring people see us, ultimately influencing our view of ourselves.

Jim Rohn, a motivational speaker, is credited with saying that we are the average of the five people we spend the most time with. Our reference group, whether it is two, five, or ten people, and the environment we are in significantly impact us. When we surround ourselves with driven and accomplished individuals, we are more inclined to embrace similar mindsets and actions. On the flip side, if we're not careful, we can adopt the attitudes and behaviors of uninspired, shallow, or time-wasting people.

Knowing how much my reference group could shape my development, I made a concerted effort to surround myself with motivated people. When I first became an entrepreneur in 2011, I sought the mentorship of more experienced entrepreneurs. I was eager to ask questions, learn from their experiences, and implement their advice into my life.

> **When we surround ourselves with driven and accomplished individuals, we are more inclined to embrace similar mindsets and actions.**

A crucial period of personal development for me occurred when I actively pursued the local Sandler Sales Franchise and successfully completed their foundational sales training, which led to my involvement in their Friday Morning President's Club, where I interacted with fellow CEOs and business professionals. Over time, this group evolved into what is now recognized as Sales Mastery. Our gatherings became one of my reference groups, solidifying my understanding of leadership, sales, and business ownership.

Within a few years, while pursuing my graduate studies, I became deeply interested in Albert Bandura's social learning theory. Bandura's experiments, such as the well-known Bobo doll study, demonstrated how people can learn new behaviors simply by observing others. During the study, kids imitated the aggressive actions displayed by adults toward the Bobo doll. Bandura's studies opened my eyes to the profound impact of social influences on human development and behavior. Consequently, I started considering how the same manner of learning through observation, as shown with research on aggression, may be applied in a positive way to assist people in improving their attitudes and behaviors.

After finishing my graduate degree in social psychology, I sought mentorship from well-known psychologists. I am currently being mentored by Norman Cotterell, a clinical psychologist renowned for his expertise in Cognitive Behavioral Therapy at the Beck Institute, and Mark Leary, a retired social and personality psychology professor from Duke University. In addition to being mentored by Norman and Mark, I also value their friendship. Through their help, I have sharpened my thinking, refined my ideas, and worked through personal challenges.

Thanks to Norman's assistance, I enhanced my mindset coaching and counseling skills, developed a more discerning ear, and adopted an empathic, evidence-based approach to helping people. With Mark's help, I have become a college professor and have acquired a deeper understanding of psychological theories and clarity about my own psychological interests and how to integrate them into my work. In all, I was able to copy and personalize their blueprints. As I observe them, I am deeply conscious of Bandura's social learning theory in a constructive light and how positive modeling can assist me in improving how I think and act.

Over time, I have absorbed *aspects* of all my mentors' viewpoints as my own. I have also imitated many of their actions—this process of observational learning has played a significant role in who I am today. When I want to take on a new challenge, such as writing this book or adopting specific traits to improve myself, I seek out individuals who have already accomplished what I want to achieve and learn from their experiences. You, too, can use this social learning method to create your *ideal self.*

In my early years as an entrepreneur, I was fascinated by the notion of being self-made, only to realize later that no one is truly self-made. We are all amalgamations of the influences others have had on us at different points in our lives, whether good or bad. As I've matured, I've learned to choose mentors thoughtfully and build my social circle with people who will positively influence my life. Like me, you can envision the kind of person you want to be and create a circle of empowerment around yourself—specific people who can inspire and assist you in becoming that person.

I am reminded of a short poem Norman shared with me about the power of positive mentors:

> The giant is strong,
> the giant is tall,
> but the dwarf on his shoulders
> sees the furthest of all.[39]

So, who is helping you to see beyond your limits? Maybe it's time to become that insightful dwarf standing on the shoulders of giants.

A Vow to Become

Your circle of empowerment is a garden. Mentors plant seeds of knowledge and advice while you and other inspiring individuals nurture the garden, leading to a bountiful harvest of personal growth. Even though these relationships are significant, the person we choose as our spouse or life partner often has the greatest effect on who we become.

I frequently say that my wife's love, encouragement, and support have played a crucial role in shaping who I am today. She has fully accepted my entrepreneurial spirit, expressed curiosity about my passions, and encouraged my personal growth. She is also a great source of advice and consistently shows her unwavering faith in me and my abilities. I am seldom angry, frustrated, or have any other negative emotions because of her.

Furthermore, she doesn't influence harmful habits that affect my well-being and shape my personality for the worse. I have never faced any obstacles from my wife in pursuing my goals, dreams, or purpose. Given the environment we've created, I'm confident she'd agree that I provide her with the same kind of support.

Numerous studies have shown that our romantic relationships significantly impact how we view ourselves and our individual attributes, whether we realize it or not. Have you ever heard someone say, "Her presence brings out the best in me," or "I am better because of him?" How often have you heard someone in a bad relationship say, "I'm unhappy with who I've become," or "I don't even recognize myself anymore."

Researchers have investigated how romantic relationships can cause people to change their sense of self in positive ways, adopting beneficial and admirable traits that lead to flourishing. They've also examined how intimate relationships influence people to change negatively, adopting undesirable and maladaptive characteristics. Studies show that our sense of self is closely connected to our romantic partners, as we become psychologically dependent on each other and see ourselves as a unit in addition to a separate individual.[40] As a result, our romantic relationships have the potential to change us in four distinct ways—*self-adulteration* and *self-contraction* fall under the category of negative changes, while positive changes encompass outcomes such as *self-pruning* and *self-expansion*.

Self-adulteration involves adding negative traits to who we are. We may acquire undesirable attitudes and behaviors because of our romantic partners' intentional or unintentional influence. In toxic relationships, a person may intensify existing negative characteristics or acquire new ones, such as smoking, drug use, excessive alcohol consumption, unhealthy eating habits, low self-esteem, emotional instability, depression, anxiety, impulsivity, and anger, among others.

Studies have shown that people are particularly likely to adopt negative traits when they strongly desire a partner who possesses those traits. These individuals tend to downplay or ignore certain negative characteristics because they want the relationship. Consequently, for the sake of the relationship, they adopt negative attributes.[40] Maybe you've heard the expression; what you allow is what will continue.

In severe situations, self-adulteration may occur when people feel controlled by their partner. Verbal and physical abuse may lead to mental health problems or cause one to behave in similarly abusive ways toward others. Hurt people *hurt* people. Not surprisingly, self-adulteration harms relationships, as people stray from their *ideal selves* and acquire undesirable characteristics.

The other way that romantic relationships can make people worse is through a process called *self-contraction*. Think about it this way: whereas self-adulteration means adopting negative traits, self-contraction means reducing the positive traits you already have. Put simply, self-contraction occurs when a person loses or decreases their positive qualities because of their romantic partner. Essentially, the good things about them start to fade away because of the unhealthy relationship, such as losing motivation, neglecting self-care, and becoming less trusting. People may also choose to ignore good friends or family just because their partner doesn't like them. They may give up on their dreams, sacrifice things they value, and suppress their feelings and emotions, seeing them as insignificant. Sadly, this negative process may also undermine positive qualities such as *honesty, virtue, humor, agreeableness, openness, sociability*, etc.[40]

People who undergo self-adulteration or self-contraction may feel less confident, which leads to insecurity. Eventually, individuals who lack independence and are being dominated by their partner grow apart from their romantic partner and become less reliant on them. So, we must be alert to detrimental changes that can occur in our romantic relationships that affect who we are and who we become. To construct our *ideal selves*, we must choose the *right* romantic partner to help us shed negative characteristics and reach our potential. It's only fair that we're ready to give them the same level of commitment.

I believe most people desire a romantic relationship that will make them a better person. I don't think anyone consciously enters a relationship with the intent of making themselves feel worse about themselves. People choose a romantic partner because they believe there's something good about that person and because of the way they make them feel—pretty, desirable, smart, or accomplished. And we all want to be recipients of something good.

Occasionally, I observe elderly married couples engaging in friendly debates over who is the more fortunate, both believing they are the luckier of the two for having found each other. In these heartwarming moments, their playful arguments make everyone around them smile. They list all the reasons why they consider themselves blessed. They believe that the other partner makes them better, which is the heartbeat of their relationship. Typically, these couples enjoy greater happiness, experience better overall health, and feel more positive about their identity. Relationships like these often involve both self-pruning and self-expansion.

Self-pruning entails eliminating undesirable characteristics because of our romantic partner's influence. The more negative traits we eliminate, our positive traits become more pronounced. Consider someone who frequently interrupts others during a conversation—this behavior may be noticed by their romantic partner, who then kindly assists them in becoming a more attentive listener. Similarly, the romantic partner may help the person identify and stop negative self-talk, resulting in a more positive attitude and higher self-esteem.

Of course, undesirable characteristics can even fade without the direct involvement of a partner. Simply being in a healthy relationship can lead people to naturally let go of negative traits that were once prominent. Furthermore, individuals may not even be aware of every specific negative attribute they have shed over time; all they know is that they're evolving into their ideal selves. As we trim away unhelpful qualities, we become better partners and reduce the likelihood of conflicts, ultimately benefiting the overall relationship.

Finally, we all find satisfaction in *self-expansion*, which involves an increase in positive qualities within ourselves that come about because of our romantic partner. But, as we've learned in this chapter, expanding oneself can be a solo journey of exploring new passions, gaining knowledge, broadening horizons, and honing skills to thrive in one's surroundings. The changes that I described are how we grow or decline in our romantic relationships as we integrate our significant other into our own sense of self.

Self-expansion characteristics may include increased *self-efficacy, gratitude, humility, openness, trustworthiness, virtue, dependability*, and *resilience*. In an enriching relationship, we may take on broader perspectives and begin to think more deeply. Some develop a newfound love for nature, travel, diverse cultural experiences, and various other activities done together with their significant other. We also have the potential to acquire greater *emotional intelligence* as we strive to please one another.

Self-expansion can also include new commitments, such as exercising, volunteering, or pursuing entrepreneurial ventures. Individuals who leave an unstable relationship may rediscover neglected interests like reading for pleasure, engaging in hobbies, pursuing education, or expressing themselves artistically. Through self-expansion, we can deepen our self-awareness, increase our sociability, and adopt a growth mindset.

Research shows that people are happier in their relationships when they help each other grow, leading to intense romantic love for one another.[40] As a result, couples have more excitement for each other and experience the novel feeling of "falling in love" more frequently, which motivates them to carry out behaviors that continue to move the relationship forward. Furthermore, people who experience self-pruning and self-expansion because of their partner are less likely to engage in emotional and sexual infidelity. Engaging in these positive self-improvement processes will increase our relationships' love, satisfaction, and commitment and help us become our *ideal selves*.

Although I have described the processes by which we become better or worse in romantic relationships, the practical outcomes are not always straightforward. People can improve in some areas while deteriorating in others because of their romantic partner. Nevertheless, we must always be aware of how strongly our relationships influence who we become. Choosing a spouse or life partner is a crucial decision that greatly impacts our *future selves*. As such, our vows *inherently* include who we will become when we commit to our romantic partner.

According to *self-discrepancy theory*, we hold beliefs about who we are, who we would like to be, and who we ought to be. Our *actual self* is who we believe we are, whereas our *ideal self* represents our hopes and dreams, and our *ought self* reflects our responsibilities and moral obligations. When we perceive a gap between our actual and ideal or ought selves, we experience emotional consequences such as disappointment and guilt.[16] Ultimately, our goal should be to achieve *self-congruence*, in which our actual self closely resembles our ideal and ought selves, resulting in greater feelings of satisfaction and well-being. It's worth noting that some degree of discrepancy is normal and can motivate personal development.

The ability to construct our best selves is the power of human agency. Simply put, we have the freedom and capability to make moral choices and contemplate our thoughts, emotions, behaviors, motivations, and desires. We can demonstrate *nimbleness* and act accordingly to achieve our goals. Animals, like dogs for example, will never decide to run laps around the neighborhood or cut back on carbs to get in shape, nor will they volunteer for training to enhance their mental abilities.

People can plan and communicate complex ideas, create and transmit culture, accumulate knowledge, and experience a wide range of emotions that we can express and interpret through various means, including language, art, and music. We are inherently curious and innovative problem-solvers, driven to explore and understand the world, leading to scientific inquiry, technological advancements, and a continuous quest for knowledge. We can also overcome adversity, accomplish remarkable feats, fight for what we believe in, and seek justice, such as civil rights leaders fighting systemic oppression. Because of human agency, we can transform ourselves, effect positive change in our communities, and make meaningful contributions to the world.

Undoubtedly, we are a unique species capable of adapting to our world, creating and shaping it in ways that distinguish us from other living organisms. Thus, failing to utilize our unique abilities fully can lead to our most significant failure, considering the power that has been bestowed upon us. Constructing who we become is the most crucial task we face because our lives are intertwined with others, and we can influence the direction of their lives. As a result, our ability to start a chain reaction in society, where our actions can help others thrive or cause them harm, is both an incredible opportunity and a tremendous responsibility. We must recognize the impact of our actions and strive to be transformative agents of positive change. In this final chapter, I will help you explore and uncover a deep-seated purpose to guide you as you design and create your ideal self.

Chapter Five Reflection Questions
Constructing Yourself Exercise

As the psychologist Elliot Aronson pointed out, "Who am I?" is a good question, but a better one is, "Who do I want to become?"

1. Who do you want to become? Describe your future self's thought process, communication style, behavior, and personality.
   a) Visualize yourself a year from now and write a paragraph about your ideal self. Then, make a list of specific traits that you admire in your newly designed self.
   b) Next, jot down three activities that you can do regularly for the next three months to nurture these qualities.
   c) Then, schedule a reminder in three months to assess your progress. At that time, you can decide to pursue three brand-new activities or continue with your current ones. You'll need to set another reminder every three months and keep the review cycle going.
   d) In a year's time, assess how closely you match the ideal version of yourself that you envisioned. Think about any challenges that have slowed down your progress and make the changes needed to overcome them. If you notice that you've started to resemble the person you described, you can likely imagine a newer version of yourself and start the entire process again.
   e) Finally, find a mentor you respect and would like to learn from. Use the same question I used to approach my latest mentors: *"I'm interested in having you as a mentor, and I have a question for you: what kind of return on investment would make you thrilled to take me on as a mentee? I'd love to learn more about that. Would it be possible to schedule a brief call to explore this further?"*

It is important to acknowledge the work associated with the *Narrative Audit* and the *Constructing Yourself Exercise.* Remember, however, that the self is not something we find but something we construct. Therefore, we must be deliberate about who we become, which requires intentional effort.

Once you gain momentum, feel free to adapt the Narrative Audit and Constructing Yourself Exercise to suit your preference and continue to apply them when you feel stuck during different stages of life. Nonetheless, I recommend keeping the core principles at the forefront of your mind and being constantly aware of how you are shaping yourself.

6

Becoming a Transformative Agent

A Life Worth Living

Many years ago, I tuned in to a popular TV show featuring high-ranking leaders disguising themselves as ordinary employees in their own companies. Usually, they uncover issues within their organization, such as ineffective processes or staff members who don't uphold the company's values. Most often, they find unnoticed employees who, despite facing difficult circumstances, demonstrate outstanding qualities and dedication that positively represent the company, leaving an impression on the undercover boss. At the end of each show, the boss reveals their real identity, which is often emotional as they address the problems and reward the deserving team members.

After watching this particular episode, I was surprised to learn that the undercover boss, Jeff, lived in my home city of Charlotte, North Carolina. I reached out to him through LinkedIn and offered to buy him coffee or lunch to see if he would mentor me. Instead, Jeff invited me to his office. As I walked through the doors of the company he founded, observing his employees and the atmosphere, I was astonished by the opportunity.

Jeff and I settled on a couch in the lounge and engaged in conversation. He asked a series of questions that eventually merged into one: "DeAngelo, why do you want to do this mentorship thing? Why do you get out of bed in the morning? Why do you do anything at all?" I looked him in the eyes and said, "Jeff, if God gives me a long life and I don't have an impact, then that would be a waste of my life. But if God gives me a long life with impact, I'd feel ready to meet him." Jeff paused as if my response had caught him off guard. After further discussion, we agreed to meet weekly for three months.

In my reply to Jeff, I expressed what I believe makes life meaningful, underscoring that God is the author of life and that we are responsible for contributing positively to the world for receiving this gift. When it comes to the question of how people *should* live and what constitutes the proper goals of human existence, psychology plays a minimal role. The social sciences focus primarily on observing and explaining current behaviors and phenomena rather than prescribing *ideal* ways of living. These moral ideas are found in the realms of philosophy and theology.

Many ancient philosophers grappled with questions concerning human flourishing, morality, and pursuing a meaningful existence. According to Socrates, "The unexamined life is not worth living."[41] Aristippus, a Greek philosopher from Cyrene in the 4th century BC, was a student of Socrates. He emphasized that pursuing pleasure was the ultimate good and most admirable way to live one's life. On the other hand, Aristotle opposed the notion that pursuing pleasure should be the ultimate goal of a meaningful life.

In Aristotle's view, everything in the world was working toward a *telos*, an ultimate end or purpose. Whether something is good or bad depends on how well it fulfills its intended purpose. Take a knife, for instance. Its purpose is to cut, so when it fulfills that function effectively, it is doing what it was designed to do. Similarly, Aristotle believed that human beings have a specific purpose, which he referred to as *eudaimonia.*

Eudaimonia goes beyond momentary happiness or pleasure. Instead, it represents a deep and lasting sense of human fulfillment achieved through a life of *virtue* or *excellence.* Aristotle's virtue ethics emphasizes character development and pursuing virtuous living rather than focusing on outcomes, strict moral laws, or rule-based behavior. Instead of asking, "What should we do?" virtue ethics concerns what *kind* of person we should be. Just as a knife's effectiveness is determined by its cutting ability, a person's goodness is defined by virtue, which is human nature's fundamental quality. In other words, virtue is a character trait that makes people better. Aristotle believed that living a virtuous life was the only way to obtain eudaimonia, which is essential to our *telos* (or purpose) as human beings.

Eudaimonia is an ethical approach to *human flourishing* and involves the development of one's human capacities, cultivating virtues, and pursuing a harmonious and ethical life within a community. As such, eudaimonia embodies a life of purpose and meaning, where individuals strive for excellence and contribute to their well-being and society. From Aristotle's perspective, eudaimonia is the key to happiness and a prerequisite for living a good life.[42]

Aristotle's virtue ethics has given me inspiration for who I am becoming. Although I can't go into detail here, he divided virtue into two categories: one that concerns our *thinking* and the other, *character.* Gaining practical wisdom, a *virtue of thinking* enables me to accurately assess situations and understand how to practice the best character virtues, such as humility, generosity, and courage, while also considering the ultimate standards of what is right.

I spend a lot of time analyzing my thoughts and actions, making it a point to read daily to expand my mind. Also, I frequently reflect on and strive to improve my character traits. To achieve my telos (or purpose), I am committed to cultivating virtues of thinking and character. You also possess the exceptional capacity to mold your character to fulfill your *telos* as a human being.

> **We are the makers of our character, and our choices determine who we will become.**

Developing the *quality* of our character is more important than achieving a large *quantity* of accomplishments. We are the makers of our character, and our choices determine who we will become.

Aristotle's virtue ethics laid the groundwork for Martin Seligman's development of positive psychology, which seeks to promote human strengths and well-being rather than simply treating mental illness. He integrated Aristotle's concept of eudaimonia (or flourishing) into his positive psychology approach and stressed the importance of cultivating and embodying virtues that lead to a meaningful life. By embracing this Aristotelian perspective, Seligman shifted the focus from merely alleviating suffering to promoting human thriving and resilience. As a result, his ideas led to the development of the *VIA Classification*, which was created through extensive research involving over fifty scientists. They looked across different cultures and countries to identify qualities universally recognized as the most significant aspects of human nature.[43]

The *VIA Classification of Character Strengths and Virtues* aims to help people recognize and develop their character strengths. The 24 Character Strengths are grouped under six core virtues: *wisdom, courage, humanity, justice, temperance,* and *transcendence.*[43] Ultimately, by extending Aristotle's virtue ethics into modern psychological practice through VIA, Seligman encouraged people to embrace their core values and character strengths as pathways to a meaningful life. In your pursuit of a purposeful life, I suggest exploring your unique character strengths at viacharacter.org.

As a final word on positive psychology, Martin Seligman introduced the notion of *P.E.R.M.A.* to identify key factors contributing to human flourishing and well-being. The five elements of *P.E.R.M.A.* are *Positive Emotions, Engagement, Relationships, Meaning,* and *Accomplishment.* Based on this model, our lives flourish when we maintain *positive emotions* such as joy, gratitude, hope, and inspiration. Furthermore, we feel more competent when we *engage* in activities that fully utilize our strengths and skills while providing us with a sense of flow or immersion in a task. Supportive *relationships* also enable us to feel connected and enhance our well-being. Ultimately, creating *meaning* in life adds to a more profound sense of fulfillment, while achieving goals and experiencing a sense of *accomplishment* can improve our self-esteem and life satisfaction.[44] It's worth noting that Seligman later amended his *P.E.R.M.A.* model to include optimism, which we've already discussed.

Earlier in this chapter, I pointed out that psychology is not concerned with dictating how people *should* live, prescribing *ideal* ways of living, or defining the *purpose* of human existence. These types of moral assessments involve the goals of philosophy and theology. Although Positive Psychology is rooted in Aristotle's virtue ethics, it aims to be morally neutral and mainly emphasizes people's subjective well-being. It does not advocate for a particular ideal life or prioritize one quality of life over another. Instead, its goal is to simply define what constitutes well-being, provide guidance on achieving it, and explore the outcomes of living a meaningful, well-lived life.[45]

On the other hand, my perspective is that living a meaningful, well-lived life is *better* than living a meaningless, wasteful life. As a result, everyone *should* strive to achieve their *telos.*

Purpose, which comes from the Greek word *telos*, means directing toward an intentional end, as explained in the previous chapter. One of our purposes *is* to become a fully functioning person, embodying human excellence, as Aristotle advocates. Additional purposes include utilizing our unique abilities to make a meaningful impact in the world through our work and fostering healthy spiritual lives, strong family bonds, and positive social relationships.

A while back, I had a conversation with an older gentleman who authored several books on the topic of purpose, a work I greatly respect. A mutual associate connected us, as I often talk about purpose in my speaking engagements and workshops, and had even recommended his book to others. Ten minutes into our meeting, it became evident to both of us that we held different perspectives on the concept of purpose, which sparked a spirited conversation and constructive disagreement. Despite both of us being Christians, he believed that God alone bestows purpose, and we must seek Him to find it. I had a slightly different perspective, but it forced me to think about the nuances of purpose that caused us to talk past each other.

I believe there are three distinct ways to understand the concept of purpose. It's worth noting that Aristotle presents purpose as the ultimate goal for human moral development, whereas my perspective focuses on the practical applications of purpose. For this reason, we can think of purpose as having three types: *transcendent*, *theocentric*, and *temporal*.

One of the most pressing questions in the history of philosophy is why something exists rather than nothing at all. Through the ages, philosophers have approached this question from different perspectives. Aristotle's work heavily influenced the medieval Christian philosopher and theologian Thomas Aquinas. He emphasized that God's supreme goodness is expressed by creating other beings. And that God's perfection and goodness were what drove Him (God) to share His goodness with others, demonstrating His abundant love in creating the world. Aquinas also recognized the constraints of human reason in comprehending the divine mystery. Yet, he attempted to provide a rational framework for understanding the relationship between God, creation, and the ultimate meaning of existence.[46]

The ideas of Aristotle and Aquinas have profoundly impacted my personal beliefs. Therefore, I believe in a *transcendent purpose*, which acknowledges God's intentional hand in creation, including the universe and everything within it. I'm also convinced that God has a plan for humankind. We are unable to control or alter God's transcendent purpose, as it is derived from His self-existing nature. This existence of a higher purpose serves as the foundation for all other purposes, anchoring the reality of purpose itself.

Transcendent purpose is a complex topic that I am unable to explore in the scope of this book. Nonetheless, my main point is that the universe and all living things display intricate designs, suggesting the existence of an intelligent designer. As a result, designed entities are intended for a specific purpose, and all living beings inherit this capacity to design with purpose.

Most people are aware of Mother Teresa's selfless service to society. She exemplifies *theocentric purpose,* a God-centered mission, or a *sense of calling* to make a difference in the world. When asked about her personal history, she said: "By blood, I am Albanian. By citizenship, an Indian. By faith, I am a Catholic nun. As to my calling, I belong to the world. As to my heart, I belong entirely to the Heart of Jesus."[47]

Mother Teresa devoted her life to serving the poor and sick in India, where she founded the Missionaries of Charity, caring for people suffering from leprosy, tuberculosis, and other diseases. Her mission was to give hope and dignity to those marginalized or forgotten by society. She believed that everyone, regardless of their circumstances or background, deserved to be treated with love and respect. Mother Teresa also lived among the poor her entire life, tending to their physical needs while providing emotional support and spiritual guidance. Her commitment to assisting others inspired countless people worldwide to join her cause and work to alleviate suffering in their communities. She is a powerful example of how one person's unwavering dedication can have a profound impact on the lives of others. We learn from her theocentric purpose that individuals who live out their unique *calling* can bring light into humanity's darkest corners and that true fulfillment comes from loving and serving others. Nevertheless, it's important to remember that, as the Senegalese proverb says, "the opportunity that God sends does not wake up those who are asleep."

Finally, as I navigate the world, I am fascinated by the innovative solutions human beings create to address various needs. Whether it's a towering skyscraper that houses hundreds of people or a sleek electric car designed to reduce emissions, I am drawn to the sheer ingenuity behind these creations. Even something as simple as a bird's nest captures my attention, as it represents a bird's solution to providing shelter and safety for egg-laying and warming their young. As such, all living beings express *temporal purpose*, which is woven into their essence. However, people have superior abilities to purposefully direct things, driven by our curiosity and imagination and executed through our rational abilities. Whether animals or people, temporal purpose can be expressed through our innate ability to direct things toward an intentional end, which exists independently of a belief in God or spiritual motives.

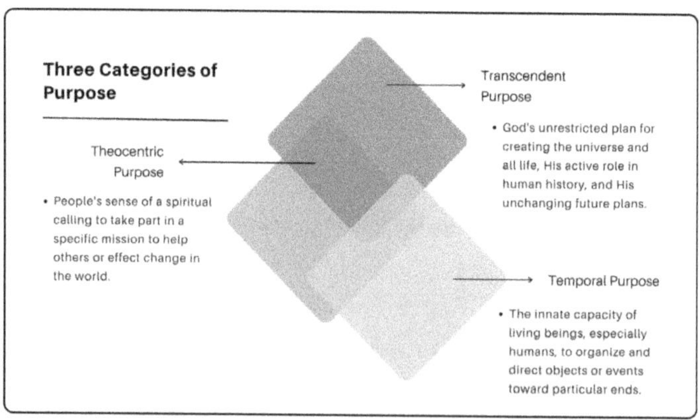

Figure 6.1 - Three Categories of Purpose

What constitutes a well-lived life is one of history's most important questions because it has direct implications for the quality of our lives. Having a sense of purpose is important for living a good life. I recognize that certain individuals face external circumstances that can impact their well-being. Even so, most of us have considerable power over how our lives unfold. We all must wrestle with the choice: to live a life without impact, fueled by selfish desire, or to live a more meaningful life spent pursuing human flourishing and mutual benefit, as I implied in my response to Jeff, the undercover boss.

My definition of a meaningful life is one in which we strive to maximize our human capacities, including developing character and intellectual virtues. Living well encompasses human flourishing that is intertwined with our personal experiences and meaningful relationships. Furthermore, it involves accepting the role of God in our lives, displaying His kindness to others, upholding good moral behavior, and making our communities and the world a better place. Overall, living with purpose, being *nimble*, and embracing positive qualities that contribute to our personal growth are essential for living a fulfilling life.

Finding Your STAR

It's a reasonable assumption that living well involves engaging in work that gives us a sense of purpose and significance. As human beings, we have an inherent inclination toward work, driven by our innate tendency to pursue goals. Whenever I give a talk on purpose, I see this desire for meaningful work. Some people ask me how to discover their purpose, while others express their frustration and unfulfillment despite all the work they put into finding and investing in their purpose. Perhaps, in an attempt to simplify things for others, speakers and writers like me have unintentionally turned the pursuit of purposeful careers into a complex puzzle. It might be wiser to shift our language from finding our purpose to *finding our STAR* when discussing a meaningful career. But more on that in a moment.

Self-Determination Theory is a scientifically supported model that explores human motivation and personality. Key to the theory is the distinction between autonomous and controlled motivation.[48] *Intrinsic motivation* is the inner drive and enthusiasm that compels us to pursue our goals and engage in activities for the pure pleasure and fulfillment they bring. This type of motivation, which promotes long-term career fulfillment and happiness, originates from within the person as opposed to being created by external rewards and punishments. When we are intrinsically motivated, we are more likely to experience a sense of autonomy, competence, and relatedness—key psychological needs identified by Self-Determination Theory that contribute to overall well-being.

Pursuing intrinsic motivation has been instrumental in shaping my career journey. Instead of only concentrating on *perceived* external markers of success, such as money, I have pursued career paths that align with my passions and personal values that bring me joy. Knowing the value of intrinsic motivation for career fulfillment, I've cultivated a strong connection between what I do professionally and who I am personally—resulting in a life of meaning and contentment.

Like me, you can embrace intrinsic motivation as the primary driving force behind your professional endeavors, leading to a more fulfilling career path. We can tap into this inner source, making us less vulnerable to external influences or temporary setbacks. By understanding what truly motivates us from within, we can create an environment where our passion drives our productivity and our creativity thrives.

In addition to intrinsic motivation, another factor that can assist us in discovering fulfilling work is choosing a profession in which we can completely immerse ourselves. Mihaly

Csikszentmihalyi was a renowned Hungarian American psychologist well-known for his groundbreaking work on the experience of *flow*. His extensive research on flow has provided valuable insights into understanding human motivation, creativity, and happiness. His work also offers practical strategies for cultivating moments of fulfillment and optimal experiences in our daily lives, illuminating how we can maximize our performance.[49]

Flow is a psychological state in which people become completely absorbed and engaged in an activity, experiencing heightened focus and enjoyment. When we are in flow, time seems to stop, and the mind shifts from conscious to nonconscious, arriving at an intuitive, creative state where our talents and skills are at their peak with maximum productivity. When we engage in activities that match our skills with the right level of challenge, we are more likely to experience flow. Clear goals and immediate feedback are also essential for flow to occur. Educators, athletes, artists, and professionals across a variety of fields have benefited from Csikszentmihalyi's work by recognizing the importance of flow in their performance and well-being.

Intrinsic motivation and flow both help to promote fulfilling careers. In musician terms, they are responsible for helping us become one with the music. As a result, it is critical to choose careers that align with our interests, values, and abilities. Additionally, we must ensure that we have suitable environments and tasks that meet the primary conditions, enabling us to experience flow states more frequently.

Rather than searching for a singular purpose, I believe guiding people toward fulfilling careers is more beneficial by helping them identify their *STAR* since both flow and intrinsic motivation are included in it. I created the acrostic S.T.A.R. to represent **S**atisfaction, **T**raining, **A**ttention, and **R**ecognition.

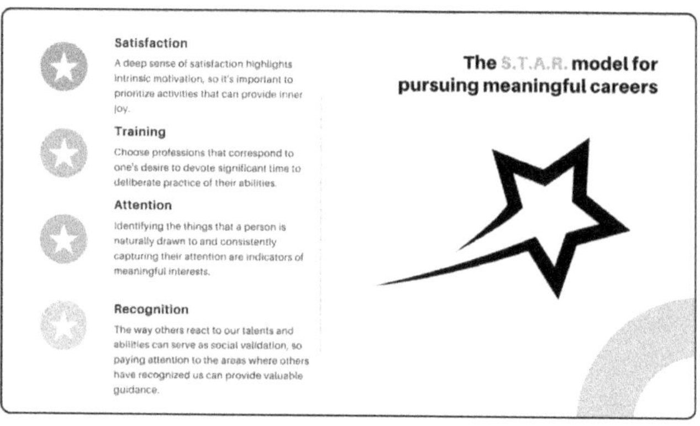

Figure 6.2 - The S.T.A.R. Model

Satisfaction is an essential part of being a happy and healthy person. In addition to affecting our feelings, actions, and overall health, the desire to be satisfied motivates us to look for relationships, jobs, experiences, and other outcomes that bring us joy. We constantly strive for a sense of contentment and fulfillment in various facets of our lives. Researchers agree that joy comes from within, not from material wealth or approval from others.[50] Although satisfaction and joy may be expressed differently, they frequently overlap and impact each other, with satisfaction often appearing before or alongside joy.

S—In locating your *STAR,* think about what brings you true *satisfaction.* You must delve deeply into your psychological needs and underlying motivations that drive you to seek fulfillment and satisfaction. These can include a wide range of human experiences, such as *achievement, affiliation, autonomy, power,* and *nurturance.* For example, a strong desire for achievement can lead people to thrive in high-reward environments. Affiliation, on the other hand, motivates individuals to seek surroundings where they can form meaningful connections and receive support from others. Autonomy enables people to assert their independence and make choices that align with their values. At the same time, the drive for power motivates individuals to seek influence and control over their surroundings, including other people. Lastly, the desire to nurture compels individuals to care for and support others, thriving in environments of compassion and empathy. Gaining insight into your psychological needs and motives can lead you to identify what truly fulfills you, ultimately pinpointing a meaningful career direction.

Angela Duckworth's concept of *grit* is also pertinent to having a satisfying career. She emphasizes that success isn't just about talent or intelligence but also about perseverance and passion.[51] In this context, deliberate training plays a critical role in developing grit. Instead of relying on abilities alone, *deliberate training* emphasizes consistent and purposeful practice. It involves setting specific, challenging goals that push us beyond our *perceived* comfort zones to cultivate skills and achieve long-term success. When we work consistently to hone our abilities, we can develop resilience and determination, cultivating a growth mindset that regards challenges as opportunities rather than barriers.

T—*Training* is an integral part of finding your *STAR*. Think about the things you are already good at, such as your natural talents or skills for which you are intrinsically motivated to practice. Which career would best enable you to hone these abilities and achieve mastery? Once you know your inherent abilities and what you enjoy, further training can lead to a more fulfilling career path.

A—Let's move on to the matter of our *attention*. Do you constantly think about a particular type of work or a unique vision? I go to bed and wake up thinking about how my work makes a difference in the world. It also consumes much of my attention throughout the day.

Attention works as a filter, selecting which information from the environment and our own storehouse of thoughts is processed further and ignored. Our thinking and actions are typically influenced by the things that capture our attention. The more attention something receives, the more power it has to influence our attitudes and steer our behaviors. Therefore, as much as possible, we must manage our focus to align with our values and goals. Recognizing what captures our *attention* is another step in discovering our *STAR*. When we identify what naturally draws our interest, we can make informed decisions about the type of work that will bring us happiness and satisfaction. However, if you're struggling to identify what consistently holds your interest, consider how your values and skills might ignite a passion you can concentrate on.

Another point: people often tell me their goals and ask for advice on achieving them. However, their aspirations seem to lose significance and fade over time. Our dreams must be meaningful enough to hold our attention hostage. Remember, what we focus on shapes our thoughts and actions.

> **Our dreams must be meaningful enough to hold our attention hostage.**

R—Finally, *recognition*. Often, others may recognize our distinct abilities in a particular area and make encouraging remarks about our competencies. Most of us can distinguish between a talented singer and a bad one, an elite athlete and a beginner, a skilled woodworker and an inexperienced one. TV shows like American Idol and America's Got Talent have long been popular, allowing us to watch those with exceptional talents while giggling at those who fall short.

In a previous chapter, I mentioned that I became interested in philosophy after someone noticed my natural aptitude for philosophical reasoning when I was younger. People around us have a way of recognizing our strengths and may validate our abilities. However, some folks also undermine our skills and bring us down, sometimes for selfish reasons, so we must be aware and have a realistic conviction about our talents. Nonetheless, most people can discern a specific defining quality in you. And most likely, it will validate what you currently understand about yourself. The ways in which others confirm our talents and skills can help us recognize meaningful opportunities that match those abilities.

To find a meaningful career path, we must first identify our personal needs, interests, talents, strengths, and personality characteristics, then look for our *STAR*! Keep in mind that although your career trajectory may shift, your *STAR* will likely remain constant. Careers are just different ways for our skills and talents to shine. Therefore, moving on from a particular position or occupation may be expected as we develop and expand. The bottom line is this: our *STAR* is the thing that brings us genuine *satisfaction*, to which we are willing to devote hours of deliberate *training*. It consumes our *attention* and is *recognized* by others as our strength or area in which we excel. Our *STAR* is where we discover purpose in our professional endeavors.

The Power of One

My guiding *STAR* led me to Charlotte, North Carolina, to pursue a degree in philosophy and theology. My desire to learn from Norman Geisler compelled me to uproot my life in Nashville, as did many others. He was an expert in Thomistic philosophy, based on the teachings of Thomas Aquinas. His profound intellect and skillful application of logic in addressing matters of reason and faith gave me a wealth of insight. His remarkable achievements, including authoring over 100 books and establishing two college institutions, inspired me deeply.

I directly interacted with Norm within a year of my arrival on campus. I enrolled in two of his courses, and after a while, I asked him for more one-on-one time. We met at his house once weekly for about six months, discussing philosophy and theological issues. I even brought my daughter on one occasion when she was five, during the time of her brain tumor, and he prayed for her. I also accompanied him to a few of his speaking engagements. Dr. Geisler was incredibly approachable for someone of his stature, and I had the privilege of getting to know some of his family members, including his lovely wife, Barbara.

After a year of being around Norm, I wondered why no one had ever documented his life in a film. At that moment, I felt a subtle nudge from God, indicating that I would be entrusted with capturing it. As a young man with rough edges, I initially confided in just one person, and I dismissed the idea in disbelief, questioning my qualifications for such a task.

Years later, I became an entrepreneur, and after seeing the imminent demise of my first business venture, I founded a new firm: a video production company. You might be making the connection now. Getting to the point, I met Norm's son at a conference, and we became close friends for a while. I even joined Norm's ministry, which built on his work. During one of our meetings, Norm's son asked me to create a video that involved Norm addressing a theological issue, which I declined. I then pitched the idea I had held on to for ten years regarding Norm's film. Upon hearing my vision, he broke down in tears right there in the restaurant.

After I completed some preliminary work, we pitched the idea to Norm. When he saw how much money we needed to raise from supporters to fund the project, Norm said, "No." He didn't want that money spent on him. Sadly, during that year, Norm suffered a stroke, which pressured us to run the idea by him again. I told him, "I wanted to give him flowers while he could still smell them." Finally, he said, "Yes."

I worked diligently, assembling a crew that included those already on my team and contracting videographers and editors affiliated with the Billy Graham Association. In addition to conducting interviews locally, I also traveled to Texas and California. I was overcome with gratitude as I spoke with numerous scholars, all of whom owed much of their work, ideas, and success to Norm's influence. I learned firsthand that I was only *one* of many whom Norm mentored, all touched by *the power of one.*

Despite significant progress, I encountered certain obstacles midway that compelled me to withdraw from the project. Nonetheless, I was able to pay tribute to my teacher, who has inspired thousands of people just like me. And I am truly honored to have played such a role despite feeling so *unqualified* when I first received the vision. It brings me great joy to know that Norm could see some of this work before he died, and you can see the movie now if you search *Norm Geisler: Not Qualified.*

We often underestimate our ability to make a positive difference in the world. Norm once told me that he never imagined becoming an author and writing more than a hundred books, considering he had grown up illiterate. And he didn't anticipate he'd become a world-renowned scholar. I also didn't believe I could inspire and bring a film to fruition. Moreover, having grown up believing I wasn't smart, I never expected to become a psychology professor and author of this book. Norm's life has taught me that I should never let feelings of inadequacy prevent me from pursuing the work I'm passionate about and that I should trust that a greater power is at work within me. You, too, can learn from this example. Belief in something bigger than ourselves can often push us beyond our perceived limits.

The measure of our power lies in our ability to make a positive difference in the lives of others, which is evident through selfless acts of service rather than solely pursuing personal gain. As we design a more meaningful life, our focus should not only be on ourselves but also on how we

> **The measure of our power lies in our ability to make a positive difference in the lives of others, which is evident through selfless acts of service rather than solely pursuing personal gain.**

can help others. Imagine me keeping all the information in this book to myself and never writing or sharing it with others. Wouldn't that have been a tremendous waste?

The primary purpose of building a meaningful life should be to empower others to do the same and reap the benefits of its positive impact. Most people prefer a healthy, flourishing society, but it should go without saying that society is made up of people. As a result, an important factor in a thriving society lies in the well-being of its individuals. And we all possess the ability to make a difference in the lives of those around us.

People have the greatest intrinsic worth; nothing in the world is more valuable, a fact that is often overlooked. Hence, there is no better investment of our time, energy, and money than to invest in people. We must, however, face the reality that individuals who possess inherent worth can also cause significant harm to us. Thus, prioritizing the needs of others does not mean we have to be pushovers or doormats.

I am astounded by the realization that every individual has a unique mind, a truly one-of-a-kind personality, exclusive emotional experiences, private memories, and a personal interaction with the world that is entirely their own. Therefore, when interacting with others, it's important to recognize that each person is uniquely special, even if they don't realize it themselves. There will *never* be another person like them, just as there will *never* be another you. Isn't that an interesting concept of scarcity? It's sad how we cherish and value rare things in society, but it's not so when it comes to people.

We must shift our *excessive* focus away from ourselves and make room for others, which involves having respect, empathy, caring, and appreciation for them. Research indicates that when we establish compassionate goals and strive to enhance the well-being of others, we often experience a boost in our own self-esteem.[52]

Since people have inherent value, assisting them in reaching their potential is worthwhile. Every mentor I've had has contributed to my growth for the sole purpose of paying it forward. Therefore, I'm following in their footsteps, participating in the timeless human tradition of rewarding one person's kindness by passing it on to others instead of just repaying the original giver. You, too, can help others along their journey by sharing what you've learned from this book.

Consider this: During middle adulthood, we begin to contemplate our impact on family, community, and society, as suggested by the late renowned psychologist Erik Erikson. As we enter this stage, introspection can lead to a sense of fulfillment and satisfaction about what we've passed on to future generations or to feelings of stagnation and disappointment.[53] Regardless of our age, striving to become the person we aspire to be is essential, as this will not only impact *what* we pass on to others but also greatly influence our future satisfaction about *how* we've lived our lives.

We have all witnessed the *power of one* person and their impact on the world, whether directly or indirectly. As this book concludes, I wanted to end with a snapshot of three people who have profoundly influenced my life and left a lasting impact on the world: Mahatma Gandhi, Martin Luther King Jr., and Nelson Mandela. These three iconic figures shared a common dedication to nonviolent resistance and social justice, influencing movements for equality and freedom around the globe.

Mahatma Gandhi, known as the father of nonviolent resistance, led India to independence from British rule through peaceful protests and civil disobedience. His philosophy of Satyagraha, or truth force, inspired countless activists and leaders to strive for change through nonviolent means. Martin Luther King Jr., deeply influenced by Gandhi's teachings, became a prominent figure in the American civil rights movement. His powerful speeches and unwavering commitment to equality ignited hope among marginalized communities and brought attention to systemic racism in the United States. King's legacy continues to inspire movements for racial justice worldwide.

Similarly, Nelson Mandela's steadfast dedication to dismantling apartheid in South Africa demonstrated the transformative power of forgiveness and reconciliation. Despite enduring 27 years of imprisonment, Mandela emerged as a symbol of unity and equality upon his release, eventually becoming South Africa's first black president. Together with Gandhi and King, Mandela stands as an example of how *the power of one* can bring about monumental societal change.

Our focus shouldn't be limited to the achievements of famous historical figures. There are also remarkable individuals in our communities who are doing extraordinary things. Cyril Prabhu, for example, lives in the Charlotte, North Carolina area, where I also reside. He founded Proverbs226 in response to his experience as a crime victim. Proverbs226 is a non-profit organization dedicated to supporting families impacted by parental incarceration through evidence-based interventions. Their mission is to disrupt the cycle of generational incarceration and unlock the potential in every child by equipping them with what they need to pursue long-term career opportunities.

Cyril saw that prison was not just breaking up families but destroying the core of what it means to be a family. Observing the perpetual impact that prison has on individuals motivated him to act. His data suggests that children of incarcerated parents have more than an 80% chance of being incarcerated at some point in their lives. Cyril believes that fostering reconciliation between parents and children will help to break the cycle.

Cyril's ministry is addressing a pressing problem: 1 out of 4 students with parents in prison will drop out of high school, and 70% of released inmates end up back in prison. Additionally, the country spends hundreds of billions of dollars annually on incarceration. Nonetheless, every child who has completed their program successfully graduated from high school. Also, after their release, every mother who participated in the program avoided reentering prison. Lastly, according to Proverbs226, the country will save one million dollars for every five children who attend college instead of ending up in prison.

Cyril also demonstrates the *power of one*! If you observe your surroundings, you will also notice others engaging in remarkable work. Such works transcend the individual and possess the ability to leave enduring legacies for future generations. Never forget, though, that you also have unique contributions to make to leave a big impact on the world. With the insights you have gained from this book, you are now equipped to help others identify the undetected influences that have shaped who they are today and guide them in becoming architects of their own lives. The responsibility now rests with you to *design* who you want to be and then pass on the knowledge. Don't underestimate your ability to become someone extraordinary and achieve something remarkable. By the same token, don't hesitate to get involved in the *seemingly* small things; you might motivate someone like me to choose a new path in life, just like my former mentor Darrell did.

Beyond Small Talk

Within the pages of this book, I have revealed elements of my life that have helped shape who I am. I have also described how I navigated through life, using my *nimble* abilities to become the person I desired to be. As I cultivated and established a more meaningful way of existing, I realized that my perceived barrier was merely a construct of my imagination, one that I could overcome. Norman Geisler once told me that you can learn more from the errors of a great mind than from the truths of a small mind—this is because great minds tend to grapple with the complexities of life, risking the possibility of overlooking an element of truth. In contrast, small minds are content with small talk.

A long time ago, I decided I wanted to design my life with the help of great minds, listen to their advice, learn from their mistakes, and constantly reevaluate my approach. In Hegel's dialectical method, history and human thought go through a series of conflicting stages but eventually reach higher levels of truth and understanding. The process of *thesis*, *antithesis*, and *synthesis* involves bringing together *different* ideas that may be imperfect or incorrect to create a new, more complete view. Drawing on Hegel's ideas, I have leveraged the wisdom of others to cultivate a more well-rounded understanding of what gives my life meaning despite not always agreeing with every perspective. You may also find yourself in a similar position, as there may be certain points that I've made with which you disagree. Nevertheless, instead of rejecting my ideas, consider how you can use the information I've provided to build a more purposeful life for yourself and others.

Considering a popular cultural idiom, I remember when the Canadian rapper Drake popularized the slogan YOLO (You Only Live Once). The term became so popular that Walgreens and Macy's began to use it. It was shouted by other celebrities, printed on t-shirts, and used as a hashtag on social media. Initially, the slogan suggested that people should embrace a life filled with pleasure and fully pursue all their desires. Admittedly, the motto even inspired me to create a video series where I interviewed successful entrepreneurs. That said, the notion of YOLO reminds us of the timeless philosophical question about what constitutes a well-lived life. If you remember, living well pertains to the thriving of individuals and communities rather than just seeking pleasure.

Because "we only live once," we must take charge of our experiences. Imagine if I said that you could swim only next summer and then never *ever* again. Unless you dislike water, you'd most likely swim every day of that summer. Instead of just swimming, though, you would fully immerse yourself in the present moment of it. And given a chance, you would probably explore swimming in different bodies of water, such as pools, lakes, rivers, and oceans. You would enhance your swimming skills and develop a unique and novel experience with the water, realizing its true beauty, functional use, and potential to bring people together in meaningful ways. And once the opportunity is gone, you'll have that dreadful feeling that what was once plentiful is now lacking in your life.

Shouldn't we live each day like our last chance to swim? If my swimming analogy doesn't resonate with you, replace it with something else that does. Ultimately, we would all do whatever it takes to maximize something we cannot get back. As a result, we must approach life as if it were our final opportunity to take a swim because it truly is.

You have been bestowed with a distinct set of abilities that you can use to make a difference in the world. These talents have been customized to help you flourish and uplift others. Whether it's your capacity for deep understanding, your knack for creating captivating art, or your talent for finding innovative solutions to intricate problems, these gifts are not just for your own success but also for the betterment of society. By harnessing your talents, you have the potential to bring positivity into people's lives, motivate others, and leave a lasting impact that will continue to shape the world long after you're gone. Discussions about your work and life will no longer be *small talk*.

A Breathing Masterpiece

The power of your talents is closely tied to who you become, which determines your ability to undermine them or propel them forward. We all intuitively know there is no greater tragedy than the premature death of one's talents, as they are forever relegated to the realm of unrealized potential. That's why we say things like "wasted talent." Philosophically speaking, talents are integral aspects of our being, reflecting the essence of who we are. In psychology, talents are our natural strengths or inclinations that can contribute to our sense of purpose and fulfillment. Without a doubt, our talents are inextricably linked to what it means to be human, and they play a significant role in shaping who we are and directing our life paths. Perhaps we would all benefit from reading the *Parable of the Talents* from Matthew's Gospel, in which the master rewards faithful servants for investing and doubling their talents while condemning the one who buried his.[54]

In writing this book, my goal is to ignite a spark within you, one that empowers you to take control of your own destiny and design a life that highlights your potential. We are not simply products of our genetics and environment; we also possess the power to shape our own lives through mindful choices and deliberate actions. By embracing my concept of *nimble*, you can transcend many boundaries set by *nature* and *nurture* and become the architect of your own life.

> **By embracing my concept of nimble, you can transcend many boundaries set by nature and nurture and become the architect of your own life.**

I want to encourage you to overcome the limitations imposed by both internal and external forces, as well as to recognize your innate capacity for personal growth. By living intentionally and making purposeful decisions, you can carve a path toward fulfillment and joy while uplifting those around you. Rather than passively waiting for a meaningful life, you can actively craft it in the present moment. With this realization comes an empowering sense of agency, knowing that we all have the capacity not only to shape our own future but also to impact the well-being of others positively through our actions. Let me leave you with these words of inspiration:

We are all painters; everyone has a canvas. Everyone is painting who they are on the world stage. Not all canvases start out equally, and none start out blank. Many canvases start out blemished and marred, and then, after intense preparation and focus by the painter, a beautiful masterpiece arises. Other canvases begin with a measure of beauty, and then after passivism and neglect by the painter, a grotesque picture arises. No matter the canvas's start, the painting's end results are found in the mind and effort of the painter, not entirely in their circumstances.

As you may have already discovered, your life is your unique canvas, and you are currently the artist behind the painting. Out of all the paintings that have been artistically rendered throughout human history, nothing even comes close to the magnitude and importance of your individual canvas. Your canvas is invaluable and cannot be auctioned off. Your canvas will outlast your existence here on Earth. Similar to how the legacies of Leonardo da Vinci, Pablo Picasso, Michelangelo, and Raphael endured long after their passing, your unique artistic creation will also survive in the memories of those who knew you.

Imagine standing on the world stage at the end of your life's journey. It's time to unveil your masterpiece to the world and take a bow. Are you prepared for your big moment? If not, take inspiration from this book and keep painting. You still have time!

Chapter Six Reflection Questions

1. Let's find your *STAR*! Without considering finances, list five areas of interest that align with your talents and abilities and bring you genuine *satisfaction* when you engage in them. Don't overthink it; just list them off the top of your head.
    a) Organize them in a ranking from 1 to 5, with 1 representing the highest *satisfaction* and 5 representing the lowest satisfaction.
    b) Next, remove items 3, 4, and 5, leaving only 1 and 2.
    c) Regarding items 1 and 2, which one are you most proficient in or willing to commit a lifetime of *training* to?
    d) Out of items 1 and 2, which one appears to hold your attention the most consistently?
    e) Which of the two do people most commonly *recognize* as a distinctive gift or ability that you possess?
    f) This is your *STAR*; write it down here: ____________.

Note* To discover fulfilling careers, it's important to keep exploring various industries, companies, positions, and roles that align with your *STAR*.

2. After learning from this chapter about what constitutes a well-lived life, write a paragraph describing your understanding of it and whether your lifestyle corresponds with these ideas. Mention what you should keep doing, change, or add to achieve it. Lastly, indicate how you can stay committed and accountable to ensure you live a meaningful life.

Notes

1. Serpell M. (2013). Guest Editorial. *British journal of pain*, 7(4), 161. https://doi.org/10.1177/2049463713507019

2. Cervone, D. (2015). *Psychology: The science of person, mind, and brain.* Worth Publishers.

3. Schein, E., & Bernstein, P. (2007). *Identical strangers: A memoir of twins separated and reunited.* Random House.

4. Eaves, L., Heath, A., Martin, N., Maes, H., Neale, M., Kendler, K., Kirk, K., & Corey, L. (1999). Comparing the biological and cultural inheritance of personality and social attitudes in the Virginia 30,000 study of twins and their relatives. *Twin Research*, 2(2), 62-80. https://doi.org/10.1375/twin.2.2.62

5. Blackburn, E., & Epel, E. (2018). *The telomere effect: A revolutionary approach to living younger, healthier, longer.* Grand Central Publishing.

6. Bray, G. A. (2015). From farm to fat cell: Why aren't we all fat? *Metabolism*, 64(3), 349-353. https://doi.org/10.1016/j.metabol.2014.09.012

7. Putri, A. W., Rahman, B. I., & Daulay, S. H. (2022). Journal of English Language Teaching. *Does Personality Influence University Students' Public Speaking?*, 7(1), 018-023.

8. Larsen, R. J., & Buss, D. M. (2020). *Personality psychology: Domains of knowledge about human nature* (7th ed.). McGraw Hill.

9. McAdams, D. P. (2001). The psychology of life stories. *Review of General Psychology*, 5(2), 100-122. https://doi.org/10.1037/1089-2680.5.2.100

10. Adler, J. M. (2012). Living into the story: Agency and coherence in a longitudinal study of narrative identity development and mental health over the course of psychotherapy. *Journal of Personality and Social Psychology*, 102(2), 367-389. https://doi.org/10.1037/a0025289

11. Friedman, H. S., & Schustack, M. W. (2015). *Personality: Classic theories and modern research*. Pearson.

12. McAdams, D. P., & Dunlop, W. L. (2022). *The Person: A New Introduction to Personality Psychology* (6th ed.). Wiley

13. Dunlop, W. L., & Tracy, J. L. (2013). Sobering stories: Narratives of self-redemption predict behavioral change and improved health among recovering alcoholics. *Journal of Personality and Social Psychology*, 104(3), 576-590. https://doi.org/10.1037/a0031185

14. Aronson, E., Wilson, T. D., & Sommers, S. (2019). *Social psychology* (10th ed.). Pearson.

15. Greaves, D. A., Pinti, P., Din, S., Hickson, R., Diao, M., Lange, C., Khurana, P., Hunter, K., Tachtsidis, I., & Hamilton, A. F. (2022). Exploring theater neuroscience: Using wearable functional near-infrared spectroscopy to measure the sense of self and interpersonal coordination in professional actors. *Journal of Cognitive Neuroscience*, 34(12), 2215-2236. https://doi.org/10.1162/jocn_a_01912

16. Gilovich, T., Keltner, D., Chen, S., & Nisbett, R. E. (2023). *Social psychology* (6th ed.). W.W. Norton & Company.

17. Cartwright, M. (2023, May 5). *Narcissus*. World History Encyclopedia. https://www.worldhistory.org/Narcissus/

18. Santrock, J. W. (2023). *A topical approach to life-span development* (11th ed.). McGraw Hill.

19. Greenberg, J., Schmader, T., Arndt, J., & Landau, M. (2020). *Social psychology: The science of everyday life* (3rd ed.). Worth Publishers.

20. Kessler, R. A. (1962). The Psychological Effects of The Judicial Robe. *The Johns Hopkins University Press, 19*(1), 35-66.

21. Honderich, H. (2023, January 24). *Tyre Nichols: Memphis police beat man like 'human pinata' - lawyers.* BBC News. https://www.bbc.com/news/world-us-canada-64380466

22. Turner, J. (Director). (2022). *Tom Clancy's Jack Ryan* [Streaming television series]. Amazon Prime Video.

23. Leary, M. R. (2007). *The curse of the self: Self-awareness, egotism, and the quality of human life.* Oxford University Press.

24. Baumeister, R. F. (1998). The self. In D. T. Gilbert, S. T. Fiske, & G. Lindzey (Eds.), *Handbook of social psychology* (4th ed., Vol. 1, pp. 680–740). New York, NY: McGraw-Hill.

25. Bohlmeijer, E., Westerhof, G., Randall, W., Tromp, T., & Kenyon, G. (2011). Narrative foreclosure in later life: Preliminary considerations for a new sensitizing concept. *Journal of Aging Studies, 25*(4), 364-370. https://doi.org/10.1016/j.jaging.2011.01.003

26. Maslow, A. H. (1970a). *Motivation and personality.* New York: Harper & Row.

27. Feist, G. J., Roberts, T., & Feist, J. (2021). *Theories of personality* (10th ed.). McGraw-Hill.

28. Corey, G., Corey, M. S., & Muratori, M. (2016). *I never knew I had a choice: Explorations in personal growth.* Cengage Learning.

29. Glasser Institute for Choice Theory. (2023). GIFCT | Committed to developing tools, resources, and support for all individuals and organizations who wish to realize the benefits of practicing Choice Theory. https://wglasser.com/

30. James, W. (1983). *The Principles of Psychology*. Harvard University Press.

31. UC Santa Cruz. (2016, May 26). *Elliot Aronson: The Power of Self-Persuasion*. YouTube. https://www.youtube.com/watch?v=Q7L3zLVnhSs

32. Buber, M. (2010). *I and thou*. Martino Fine Books.

33. Dweck, C. S. (2007). *Mindset: The new psychology of success*. Ballantine Books.

34. Maxwell, J. C. (1998). *The 21 irrefutable laws of leadership*. Thomas Nelson Publishers.

35. Richter, Curt P. (1957). On the phenomenon of sudden death in animals and man. *Psychosom*. Med., 19, 191-8.

36. Camus, A. (1991). *The myth of Sisyphus and other essays*. Vintage.

37. Frankl, V. E. (2006). *Man's search for meaning*. Beacon Press.

38. Life.Church. (2023). *1 Corinthians 15*. YouVersion | The Bible App | Bible.com. https://www.bible.com/bible/111/1CO.15.NIV

39. Tripp, W. (1985). *Marguerite, go wash your feet*. Houghton Mifflin Harcourt.

40. Mattingly, B. A., Lewandowski, G. W., & McIntyre, K. P. (2014). "You make me a better/worse person": A two-dimensional model of relationship self-change. *Personal Relationships, 21*(1), 176-190. doi:10.1111/pere.12025

41. Plato, & Jowett B. (2020). *Apology*. Independently published.

42. Aristotle, & Sachs, J. (2002). *Nicomachean ethics*. Focus.

43. Niemiec, R. M., & McGrath, R. E. (2019). *The power of character strengths: Appreciate and ignite your positive personality*. VIA Institute on Character.

44. Seligman, M. E. (2011). *Flourish: A visionary new understanding of happiness and well-being*. Simon & Schuster.

45. Seligman, M.E.P. (2002). Authentic Happiness: *Using the new positive psychology to realize your potential for lasting fulfillment.* Free Press.

46. Stief, J., & Aquinas, T. (2017). *Summa Theologica: The only complete and unabridged edition in one volume.* Independently Published.

47. Cannon, Mae Elise (2013). *Just Spirituality: How Faith Practices Fuel Social Action.* InterVarsity Press. p. 19. ISBN 978-0-8308-3775-5. Archived from the original on 1 February 2022. Retrieved 3 September 2016

48. Deci, E., & Ryan, R. (2012). Self-determination theory. In *Handbook of Theories of Social Psychology*: Volume 1 (Vol. 1, pp. 416-437). SAGE Publications Ltd, https://doi.org/10.4135/9781446249215

49. Csikszentmihalyi, M. (2009). *Flow: The psychology of optimal experience.* HarperCollins.

50. Isham, A., Verfuerth, C., Armstrong, A., Elf, P., Gatersleben, B., & Jackson, T. (2022). The Problematic Role of Materialistic Values in the Pursuit of Sustainable Well-Being. *International journal of environmental research and public health*, 19(6), 3673. https://doi.org/10.3390/ijerph19063673

51. Duckworth, A. (2018). Grit: *The power of passion and perseverance.* Scribner.

52. Canevello, A., & Crocker, J. (2011). Interpersonal goals, others' regard for the self, and self-esteem: The paradoxical consequences of self-image and compassionate goals. *European Journal of Social Psychology*, 41(4), 422-434. doi:10.1002/ejsp.808

53. Feldman, R. S. (2019). *Development across the life span* (9th ed.). Pearson.

54. Bible Gateway. (2001). *The Parable of the Talents: Matthew 25:14-30 - English standard* version. https://www.biblegateway.com/passage/?search=Matthew%2025%3A14-30&version=ESV

Index

J

James, William 84
Journal of Cognitive Neuroscience
26, 134

K

Kessler, Robert A. 41
King, Martin Luther Jr. 125
King, Solomon 17, 18

L

Law of the Lid 88, 89
Leary, Mark v, 96
Lewin, Kurt 28
Looking-Glass Self 37, 38, 40, 41,
49, 50, 94

M

Mandela, Nelson 125, 126
Maslow, Abraham 61, 79
Maxwell, John 88
McAdams, Dan 33
Meaning-Why-Purpose Analysis 92
Mental Illness 8, 10, 110
Meta-Narratives 21
Mindfulness-Based Cognitive
Therapy 66
Mindset Disparity 61
Misperceptions 29
Model of Relatedness 87
Mother Teresa 113

N

Narcissism 31
Narcissus 31, 32, 134

Narrative Audits 33, 66, 67, 69
Narrative Foreclosure 68, 70, 72
Narrative Identities 23, 26
Narrative Identity 19
Narrative Psychology 19
Narrative Therapy 55
Nature and Nurture 4, 6, 9, 14, 130
Nature versus Nurture 4
Negative Self-Talk 29, 30, 32, 33,
100
Neuroticism 11, 30
Nichols, Tyre 44, 48, 135
Nietzsche, Friedrich 91
Nimble 4, 14, 51, 66, 72, 80, 83,
115, 127, 130
Nimbleness 14, 102

O

Openness 11, 87, 99, 101
Ought Selves 102

P

Parable of the Talents 130, 137
PERMA 111
Personal Identity 36
Personality Traits 7, 11, 24, 88
Pessimists 29
Political attitudes 8
Prabhu, Cyril 126
Proverbs226 126, 127
Psychological Fog. See Foggy Per-
spectives 76
Purpose 19, 21, 59, 76, 79, 86, 88,
90, 91, 92, 98, 103, 109,
110, 111, 112, 113, 114,
115, 116, 117, 121, 124,
125, 129

V

W

Y

Z

DEANGELO BURSE

SUMMARY OF PROGRAM DETAILS

KEYNOTE AND WORKSHOP PRESENTATIONS

DeAngelo offers his distinctive system in various formats, including a 45 min. keynote presentation, a 90 min. workshop, a 5-hour workshop, or a 10-hour workshop. It's important to note that the 5-hour workshop is designed as a one-day event, while the 10-hour workshop spans two days.

EXECUTIVE AND LEADERSHIP COACHING

DeAngelo integrates his distinct approach into both individual and group coaching sessions, drawing from Cognitive Behavioral Coaching (CBC) to highlight the relationship between thoughts, emotions, and actions. This approach centers on resolving issues and minimizing detrimental negative thoughts and feelings. Additionally, he incorporates aspects of Reality Therapy to underscore personal accountability for decisions and encourage more positive choices for a more fulfilling life.

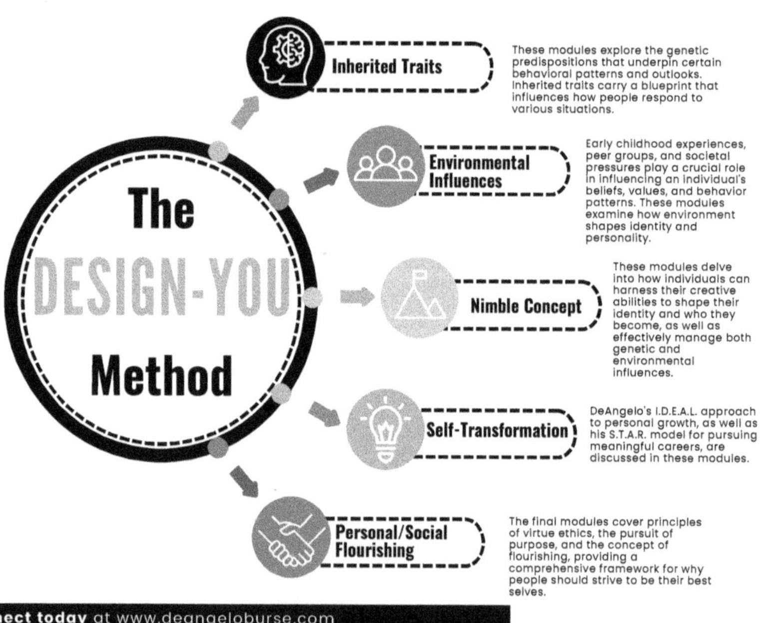